P9-DWE-644

DATE DUE

DE 7 '99			
DE 01 '02			
DE 7 '04			
OC 27 '06			

DEMCO 38-296

Drug-Free Youth

GARLAND REFERENCE LIBRARY OF SOCIAL SCIENCE
VOLUME 1038

DRUG-FREE YOUTH
A COMPENDIUM
FOR PREVENTION SPECIALISTS

EDITED BY
ELAINE NORMAN

GARLAND PUBLISHING, INC.
NEW YORK AND LONDON
1997

Riverside Community College
Library
4800 Magnolia Avenue
Riverside, California 92506

HV 5824 .Y68 D7735 1997

Drug-free youth

Copyright © 1997 by Elaine Norman
All rights reserved

Library of Congress Cataloging-in-Publication Data

Norman, Elaine.
    Drug-free youth : a compendium for prevention specialists /
[edited by] Elaine Norman.
        p.   cm. — (Garland reference library of social science ; v. 1038)
    Includes index.
    ISBN 0-8153-2048-5 (hardcover) (alk. paper)
    ISBN 0-8153-2047-7 (paperback)
    1. Teenagers—Drug use—United States.   2. Drug abuse—United
States—Prevention.   I. Title.   II. Series.
    HV5824.Y68N65   1997
    362.29'17'0835—dc20   96–32670
                                                           CIP

Paperback cover design by Karin Badger.

Printed on acid-free, 250-year-life paper
Manufactured in the United States of America

CONTENTS

PREFACE

There is an almost universal consensus that we as adult individuals, as communities, and as a nation, should attempt to prevent our youngsters from using alcohol, tobacco, and other drugs such as marijuana, cocaine, and heroin. We, the adults, use these substances in abundance—especially the legal ones, alcohol and tobacco. Our youngsters find them readily available, and they know that they offer a number of satisfactions. They know, for example, that substance use has the potential to relieve feelings of inadequacy and other psychological pains that naturally occur with adolescence and that use offers an opportunity to express opposition to authority, to affirm solidarity with peers, and to appear "grown up" (Jessor, 1985).

Why then, if we use substances to such a large extent and if we know they offer certain satisfactions, do we wish to prevent our youngsters from partaking? The answer is obvious. As a culture we are deluged with evidence of the harmful effects of alcohol, tobacco, and other illicit drugs. We know that important risk factors for regrettable, sometimes tragic, accidents and for health problems in later life have their roots in youthful incautious substance use (Public Health Service, 1995a). We wish to protect our children from lung cancer, heart disease, cirrhosis of the liver, drunk driving accidents, and addiction.

Recognizing this we have made the use of alcohol, tobacco, and other drugs illegal before adulthood. We wish to prevent our children from beginning to use these substances until they are adults— older, more mature, and better able to make reasoned decisions.

Teen-agers do use substances in much larger numbers than we are comfortable with. In 1992, according to the National Household Survey on Drug Abuse (Public Health Service, 1995b), four out of every ten adolescents aged twelve to seventeen reported having used alcohol at least once in their life, one out of every three reported having used tobacco, and one out of every six reported having used an illicit drug (mainly marijuana). These figures have been dropping significantly since 1979. The 1979 figures are stunning in comparison to the 1992 figures we just noted. In that earlier year, seven of ten youngsters of that age reported having used alcohol, more than five in ten reported ever using tobacco, and one in three reported ever using another illicit substance. As the nation became more health conscious a steady downward trend in substance use among youth seems to have occurred (see table below).

Percent of 12- to 17-year-olds reporting ever using substance

	In 1979	In 1985	In 1992
Alcohol..................	70.3%	55.4%	39.3%
Tobacco.................	54.1%	45.3%	33.7%
Other illicit drugs	34.3%	29.7%	16.5%

Source: (Public Health Service, 1995b).

The 1992 numbers are still quite high and there is evidence that a definitely discernable rise in use among youngsters has been occurring since 1992 (Swan, 1995).

In the past decade and a half considerable public resources have been devoted to the development and testing of school and community-based programs designed to prevent substance use and abuse among adolescents. At the present time three-quarters of the school districts in the United States have anti-smoking programs, and nearly two-thirds have alcohol and other drug programs as part of their curriculum (Public Health Service, 1995a). Some such programs have been proven to be effective prevention tools, while others have not.

For three and a half years, from 1990 to 1994, a team of researchers and clinical practitioners from Fordham University's Graduate School of Social Service, with funding from the New York State Office of Alcohol and Substance Abuse Services, worked to review the literature published in the past two decades pertaining to the content and outcomes of adolescent substance abuse prevention programs which had been fielded during that twenty-year period. The results were presented to over a thousand substance abuse prevention specialists in a series of seminars throughout New York State. Included were prevention specialists in schools and social agencies, junior high and high school teachers, social workers, and school administrators.

The magnitude of the appreciation voiced by the attendees for the material in the seminars led to the development of this book.

All of those present were working in the field, in schools and community agencies, attempting to accomplish adolescent substance abuse prevention. Most didn't have up-to-date information on the most effective strategies. They didn't know how to obtain curriculums related to those strategies nor how to get training in using them. They had little formal information on the adolescent developmental issues that might affect substance use. Few were aware of the new trends in program development such as resiliency enhancement. Even fewer were equipped to do research evaluations of their programs. Most were eager to know about funding sources to help them develop new or expand existing programs.

In order to answer those concerns, interests, and needs this book was developed. It is intended as compendium of materials to help adolescent substance abuse prevention specialists develop, improve, evaluate, and fund prevention programs.

The first chapter in the book presents a clinician's view of the developmental issues faced by adolescents that potentially affect substance use. Carol P. Kaplan notes in "Adolescent Development: Risk, Vulnerability, and Resilience," that adolescence is a period of both vibrant growth and vulnerability and risk. The vitality and emotions of adolescence can at times be misunderstood as pathological, while some seriously disturbed behavior can be misinterpreted as normal. The article helps us to understand the nature of normal adolescence and the indicators of disturbance. Knowledge of both are essential in our effort to help teen-agers avoid substance abuse.

In order to choose productive prevention programs for teenagers, it is important to know what has already been tried and found effective as well as what has proved not to be useful. In the second chapter, "Prevention Programs Reviewed: What Works?," Elaine Norman, Sandra Turner, Sharyn J. Zunz, and Kathy Stillson review the curriculum-based adolescent substance abuse prevention strategies developed in the past two decades, their theoretical underpinnings, and the outcomes of their research evaluations. The chapter describes the components of successful curriculum-based prevention programs and includes information on how to locate the program coordinators in order to obtain curriculum materials and training in their use.

Prevention efforts that are not curriculum based have also contributed to the reduction of substance use among adolescents. These include efforts to change school climate and community norms. That is the subject of chapter three by Sharyn J. Zunz. Extensive public health efforts to change community norms have been fielded. The most well known, those concerning tobacco consumption and driving while intoxicated, have had positive results nationwide as have attempts by some schools and community agencies to change their organizational climate and policies to help impart non-substance use norms to students. The chapter describes a number of these efforts in detail and includes a synthesis of useful suggestions for developing such programs for adolescents.

In recent years the field of adolescent substance abuse prevention has been undergoing a paradigm shift. Instead of focusing upon reduction of risk, vulnerability, and pathology the spotlight has turned to enhancement of strengths and resiliency. Chapters four, five, and six deal with this topic. They outline the personal, family, school, and community factors that, according to the research literature, enhance sustained competent functioning even in the presence of major life stressors. These chapters describe programs that utilize this material in their prevention efforts.

In "New Directions: Looking at Psychological Dimensions in Resiliency Enhancement," Elaine Norman reviews the theoretical underpinnings of the resiliency concept and synopsizes the research literature related to the psychological factors that make up, and enhance, resiliency. In "Building on Strengths: Risk and Resiliency in the Family, School, and Community," Sandra Turner does the same for family, school, and community resiliency factors.

Few evaluated prevention programs have targeted minority youngsters. There has also been a paucity of publications specifically related to the strengths of minority group adolescents, and the ways such strengths can be, and are, mobilized to prevent substance abuse. Saundra Murray Nettles, in "Resilience in African American Adolescents: Issues Pertinent to Alcohol and Other Substance Use," examines current misconceptions of African American adolescents' use of alcohol, tobacco, and other drugs; reviews risk and protective factors making for greater vulnerability or greater resiliency; and describes models of meaning, culture, and context relevant to resiliency enhancement prevention programming for African American youth.

Whatever substance abuse prevention program we implement we want to know if, and to what extent, it achieves its intended goals. Most funding agencies wish to know this too. Michael Phillips in "Did We Make a Difference?: Techniques and Process in Program Evaluation" leads us through all the steps one must undertake when evaluating a prevention program. From the original goal setting to the final report writing he details each stage of the research endeavor to follow in order to measure how well the program works.

Finally, conducting and evaluating adolescent substance abuse prevention programs is expensive. Although as a society we have given lip service to the need for prevention, public health and substance abuse professionals have constantly had to struggle to obtain financial support for prevention activities. From the onset of public funding in the area of substance abuse, the lion's share of governmental monies have been earmarked for law enforcement and interception of illegal drug supplies. Most of the small remaining share has been funneled into much needed addiction treatment programs, leaving very little for prevention efforts. In these days of shrinking resources, obtaining funding for prevention activities from outside sources has become a genuine art. In "Funding Substance Abuse Prevention Programs for Youth," Roslyn H. Chernesky discusses funding opportunities from foundations and from federal agencies and she gives detailed information on the grantmaking process and proposal writing.

This volume contains the most recent knowledge available in the field. The hope is that it will prove helpful as we work to assist our youth in their effort to be, and to remain, substance free.

Elaine Norman

Professor
Fordham University at Lincoln Center
Graduate School of Social Service

REFERENCES

Jessor, R. (1985). Bridging etiology and prevention in drug abuse research. *N.I.D.A.-Research Monograph Series, 56,* 257-268.

Public Health Service. (1995a). *Healthy People 2000: National Health Promotion and Disease Prevention Objectives.* U.S. Dept. of Health and Human Services. DHHS Pub. No. (PHS) 91-50213.

Public Health Service. (1995b). *National Household Survey on Drug Abuse: Main Findings 1992.* U.S. Dept. of Health and Human Services, SAMHSA, Office of Applied Studies. DHHS Pub. No. (SMA) 94-3012.

Swan, H. (March/April 1995). Marijuana and other drug use among teens continues to rise. *NIDA Notes.* U.S. Public Health Service. (NIH Pub No. 95-3478), 8-9.

CHAPTER 1

Adolescent Development: Risk, Vulnerability, and Resilience

Carol P. Kaplan

INTRODUCTION

Adolescence as a developmental phase contains certain features that can be regarded as universal. It is an eventful time with opportunities for vibrant growth as well as vulnerability and risk. Interwoven with the universal characteristics of adolescence are various constitutional factors and experiences which may influence the adolescent towards either developmental progress or dysfunction. For example, trauma and victimization, as well as social stressors such as poverty and racial discrimination, may place young people at risk (Turner et al., 1994; Garmezy, 1991; Dornbusch et al., 1991; Arnold, 1990; Gibbs et al., 1989; Rutter, 1987; Myers and King, 1983).

Drawing upon established theories as well as more recent research findings, the following chapter presents an overview of some of the ways in which we understand normal adolescent development as well as risk, vulnerability, and resilience. The chapter will examine developmental processes beginning in early childhood, and review a number of specific problems of adolescence. Substance abuse frequently accompanies both developmental dysfunction and specific disorders of adolescence, so the chapter will highlight the relationship between these issues and adolescent substance abuse in an ecosystemic framework.

NORMAL ADOLESCENT DEVELOPMENT AND VULNERABILITY

Early Childhood

Infancy and early childhood impact subsequent development greatly. Along with basic nourishment and care, children require the opportunity for attachment, or bonding, with at least one significant nurturing adult as well as continuity of care, consistency, love, and appropriate discipline. When any of these ingredients are absent or when young children are malnourished, neglected, abused, or denied the opportunity to bond because of the loss of significant caretakers, detrimental effects upon personality development and competent functioning can be expected, sometimes profound and lifelong ones (Bowlby, 1973; 1980; 1982; Spitz, 1965; Mahler et al. 1975). Many adolescents who become seriously dysfunctional or delinquent have early histories of extreme loss, deprivation, or abuse (A. Freud, 1967; Eisen, 1972; Winnicott, 1973; Marohn et al., 1982; Mishne, 1986; Goodman, 1988.)

Latency

Developmentally, early childhood is followed by the period traditionally known as latency, roughly ages 6 to 11. Because of the great importance of early childhood events, the significance of latency is not always appreciated. According to Sarnoff (1976), latency is a period of relative calm, pliability, and educability. The "average expectable environment" provides nurturing, stability, and structure and protects children from inappropriate aggression and sexual overstimulation. In such an environment they attend school and learn academic skills, while playing musical instruments, joining teams, pursuing hobbies, making friends, and in general, achieving a sense of their own capabilities and increasing their sphere of mastery (a process that would have begun during early childhood.) Thus strengthened by this period of growth, children are better able to withstand the pressures of the next phase of development: adolescence.

Children who have not been able to gain skills and mastery during latency, e.g. because of learning disabilities, a chaotic or destructive home environment, or emotional problems, will find adjustment during adolescence much more difficult (Meeks and Bernet, 1990). Unfortunately, many children in our society are at risk for substance abuse, school dropout, pregnancy, and delinquency in their teen years. Without adequate adult supervision or family supports, or in communities devastated by poverty, neglect, and violence, they are deprived of opportunities for learning and mastery. Some experts recommend school-based support services for latency-age children in order to prevent dysfunction then and during adolescence.

2 ADOLESCENT DEVELOPMENT

Adolescence

The period between childhood and adulthood, which begins with the physical changes of puberty and may have a variety of different end points, has now come to be recognized as a distinct developmental phase in all cultures (Schlegel and Barry, 1991). Adolescence brings changes in the physical, psychological, cognitive, and social spheres of an individual's life. However, there is great variability among individuals, and chronological age does not necessarily correspond to physical or emotional age.

Physical Changes

Growth may occur unevenly or in spurts, differentially for boys and girls and for different individuals. Adolescence also brings the development of reproductive capacity and secondary sexual characteristics. Girls and boys whose bodies are changing frequently become self-conscious and self-involved. Sexuality becomes an important issue. Hormonal changes and fluctuations may lead to moodiness, although this is not inevitable (Brooks-Gunn, 1991). Early maturing girls and late maturing boys seem to have special problems.

Psychological Changes

The developmental ego psychological approach to adolescence of such writers as Anna Freud (1958), Erikson (1950, 1968), Laufer (1966), and Kaplan (1984) describes the normal adolescent developmental process as a "psychosocial moratorium," with a normative identity crisis and a period of mourning and depression, during which the young person makes a final emotional separation from parents and bids farewell to childhood. This has been called the "second separation-individuation process" (Blos, 1962, 1979). The young person finally experiences himself or herself as separate from, and eventually makes a life apart from, the parental family. Acting out and experimentation are normal and even desirable, according to this theory. The optimal result will be intimacy with a partner and the development of a separate identity. Ideally, the young person will establish himself or herself in the world of work based upon individual interests, skills, and abilities to the extent that society provides adequate opportunities for employment and self-development.

In contrast to the view that adolescence inevitably is tumultuous, some writers have maintained that it need not be so (Offer, 1987).

3

While the individual (and the family) may be challenged to cope with new realities, most are able to do so. However, even those who view normal adolescence as a period of generally successful coping agree that the most stormy stage for young people is likely to be early adolescence—around ages 12 to 14—roughly the period of junior high school. This age group must manage often dramatic physical and emotional changes, including hormonal ones, within a school context with less structure than primary school provided (Miller, 1983; Peterson et al., 1991).

In addition, for young teenagers the desire for increased independence from parents comes at a time when the capacities to manage such independence are not firmly in place—a fact usually recognized by the parents and on some level by the teen as well. Irritability, emotional lability, even tantrums, may appear in this phase and then dissipate as the adolescent becomes increasingly able to cope with more independence and the challenges of high school. Clearly, during these years families will experience stress and must draw upon their adaptive abilities. If, however, parents either overreact to the young teenager and fail to establish a dialogue or do not set appropriate limits, the undesirable behavior patterns may become fixed (Offer, 1969; Miller, 1983.)

Virtually all writers on adolescence agree on the importance of the peer group. The adolescent draws close to peers just at the time when he or she confronts the fact that parents are neither perfect nor omnipotent. The peer group provides the support required during this stage of normative disillusionment and aids the teen in the tasks of separation from the parents and establishment of a new identity. Especially during the early adolescent period, young people, in their desire for acceptance, are inclined to follow the peer group in every detail of behavior and style, while at the same time they appear to be rejecting parental (and sometimes societal) values (Miller, 1983).

Obviously, therefore, the characteristics of the peer group now assume tremendous importance. Some of the classic research and writing on adolescence grew out of society's concerns about "juvenile delinquency," often defined as antisocial behavior by adolescents in groups (Aichhorn, 1963). Indeed, antisocial, underachieving, or substance abusing peers may impact very negatively upon an adolescent's trajectory towards adulthood, especially if childhood developmental accomplishments have been tenuous or deficient. Obviously, therefore, communities in which violence and substance abuse are prevalent will tend to produce more antisocial adolescents.

Paradoxically, adolescents continue to need adult attention, support, and guidance, even as they sometimes seem to be rejecting the adults in their life, and even as school structure (as well as some family structures) tends to mitigate against stable relationships with adults (Miller, 1983; Schlegel and Barry, 1991). If adults fail to recognize the fact that adolescents continue to need their guidance and support and ignore or reject the rebellious young person, negative consequences may result. Adolescents flourish in an atmosphere of dialogue and discussion (Hauser et al., 1991), which the parents may be unable to provide if they are overwhelmed or inadequate to the task of parenting.

Cognitive Changes

Adolescence marks the beginning of the capacity for abstract reasoning (Piaget, 1967; Flavell, 1963). For the first time, most young people become able to understand philosophical and ideological issues in their full complexity and to appreciate concepts like "the future" more realistically. Yet because of their new ability to think abstractly, adolescents come to see and understand problems which they did not previously perceive as such, especially in areas like future work opportunities (or the lack of them), values, and the complexity of interpersonal relationships. Thus, this very capacity for abstract thinking can create new difficulties and new challenges for coping, as the "world of what matters" (Larson and Asmussen, 1991) is expanded. The following are some examples:

1. With friends and members of the opposite sex, who are now so important, such issues as loyalty, trust, and betrayal arise for the first time and are capable of causing negative as well as positive emotions. The young person will need to call upon all of his or her resources to cope with these intense feelings.

2. As abstract reasoning allows youngsters to project themselves into the future, an opportunity is provided for some adolescents to change course and take a more positive direction. As following chapters note, a sense of self-efficacy and optimism as well as at least one positive relationship with a caring adult in the family, school, and/or the community are among the ingredients associated with resiliency and positive outcomes. In their absence, despair and dysfunction may result (Zunz et al., 1993).

3. In conjunction with the capacity for abstract reasoning, and an increased ability to experience the complexity of relationships, the adolescent may be both more empathic and more aware of ambiguity

than was the case in childhood. In the long run, this may lead to growth. In the short run, however, the individual may actually feel more vulnerable. In fact, as Norman indicates in chapter four, some research shows that a high degree of empathy may prove detrimental to teens in high stress situations.

Social Changes

From the sociological point of view, adolescence is a period of social role learning and restructuring (Schlegel and Barry, 1991). For the first time, the youngster possesses real power of independent action. In order to understand these issues, particularly as they impact upon risk and vulnerability in adolescence, a systemic, ecological point of view is extremely useful for the following reasons.

1. It is in the peer group that adolescents can rehearse the social activities and behaviors of adulthood (Schlegel and Barry, 1991). As noted above, however, certain peer groups may foster antisocial roles, leading to increased vulnerability.

2. The cognitive changes of adolescence pave the way for this learning of new social roles. Optimally they are fostered in the secondary school environment, in which adequate support is provided not only for cognitive development but for constructive social role learning as well. However, in some communities school may become the place where violence and negative social roles are rehearsed.

3. Society must foster and promote appropriate social role learning by providing opportunities for future productive work. Only if such opportunities are available do adolescents have an incentive to defer immediate gratification in preparation for a rewarding future. At least half of U.S. youth do not go to college, and many fail to graduate from high school (Petersen et al., 1991). Too many teens, especially those who are poor, see opportunities in life on the street as more attractive and financially rewarding than those in the legitimate job market. The question for many of these young people is not how to make it but whether to even try and make it (Inclan and Herron, 1989).

4. The structure of our society leads to gender specific vulnerabilities. For example, girls in adolescence may be more vulnerable to depression (Petersen et al., 1991) and to declining academic motivation (Gilligan et al., 1990), while boys may respond to stress during this period with increased acting out. Too, for girls, early puberty may produce stress, while it rarely does so for boys (Brooks-Gunn, 1991).

5. For those young people inadequately equipped during latency with the academic skills that will prepare them for productive work, adolescence may be the last opportunity for remediation. Here again, schools may not provide such remediation appropriately, and the teenager who feels like a failure may even drop out, thus foreclosing constructive options for the future.

6. It would appear that the very transitions of adolescence can cause stress for some youngsters, especially if they occur in the context of other developmental events. For example, some research suggests that young people who enter puberty at the same time that they begin junior high school may have more problems than those whose physical development occurs later—multiple changes occurring simultaneously can produce vulnerability and risk (Simmons et al., 1987).

7. Normative adolescence may look different for young people from different social backgrounds and social classes. For example, it has been pointed out that while for the middle class white adolescent in our society increasing physical and psychological separation from the family and involvement with peers can be considered appropriate and healthy, the situation is different for many Puerto Rican teens. A well-differentiated and functional adolescent in a poor Puerto Rican family, for instance, may take on great responsibility for the family unit, including the parents; while the lack of such family responsibilities and expectations tends to be associated with psychosocial dysfunction and even antisocial behavior (Inclan and Herron, 1989). This idea correlates with the finding of researchers that resilient adolescents from high-risk environments tend to have family responsibilities (Werner and Smith, 1992).

Thus, from the ecosystemic point of view, it is clear that the developments in the different spheres cited above are not really separable when we view adolescence as a period of potential risk and vulnerability as well as one of new opportunities for coping and resilience. Rather, the physical, emotional, cognitive, and social developments of adolescence all mesh with each other. The early years of life, as well as constitutional and environmental factors, provide the foundation for later relationships and overall functioning. Then, in adolescence, the world of relationships is transformed by the introduction of intimacy, and also by the increased possibilities for thinking about the complexity of relationships. As the adolescent considers the future and his or her role in life, influences from the family, school, community, and society at large will be crucial.

SPECIFIC PROBLEMS OF ADOLESCENCE

Contrary to the view held by earlier writers on adolescence that serious problems are part of the normal adolescent developmental process, research suggests that mood swings, turmoil, and serious rebellion (as opposed to moodiness, bickering, and oppositionalism) are not normative or inevitable in adolescence (Brooks-Gunn, 1991; Offer, 1987; Masterson, 1968). Rather, it appears that emotionally and behaviorally disturbed adolescents may tend to become disturbed adults. As Petersen et al. (1991) have pointed out, adolescence is a time of divergence between those on a positive developmental trajectory and those on a negative one.

Serious Psychiatric Disorders

It is in adolescence that many adults with serious psychiatric disorders present the first clear manifestations of these disorders, even though in retrospect precursors may have been evident in childhood. However, these psychiatric disorders may be difficult to diagnose because of both adolescent developmental characteristics and the complicating factor of substance abuse. Indeed, seriously disturbed adolescents are frequently seen as having "a bad case of adolescence," despite the fact that the majority of such young people go on to become disturbed adults (Masterson, 1967). The importance of recognizing these severe disturbances cannot be underestimated; proper diagnosis and treatment can prevent deterioration or ameliorate psychosocial dysfunction in later life. The following section will review the major mental disorders and their manifestations in adolescence.

I. Mood Disorders

A. BIPOLAR DISORDER. This disorder, involving severe mood swings (mania and depression) and psychosis in adulthood, rarely appears in full blown form before puberty. Even then, in many instances it is either not recognized or is misdiagnosed. Delinquency or drug abuse may divert attention from the underlying problem, or the youngster may appear either overexcited or depressed. The presence of psychotic symptoms may lead to an erroneous diagnosis of schizophrenia. Other frequent misdiagnoses include adjustment reactions and behavior or personality disorders, especially borderline personality disorder (Kaplan and Shachter, 1993; Wenning, 1990; Kron and Kestenbaum, 1988; Anthony and Scott, 1960.)

Research repeatedly points to a familial concordance in all mood disorders (Kaplan and Shachter, 1993; Rauch et al., 1991; Akiskal, 1989; Kron and Kestenbaum, 1988). When an adolescent is having problems, a history of bipolar disorder in family members, especially parents, should alert clinicians and others working with that youngster to the possibility of its existence. In childhood, i.e., prior to the onset of puberty, individuals who eventually evidence bipolar disorder may present a variety of behaviors. Some may be diagnosed with Attention Deficit/Hyperactivity Disorder (Schmidt and Friedson, 1990). Other symptoms include disruptive temper outbursts, sleep disturbance, impaired personal relationships, extreme moodiness, antisocial or aggressive behavior, grandiosity, difficulty keeping friends, and controlling and demanding behavior (Kaplan and Shachter, 1993).

While bipolar disorder cannot currently be predicted, it is important to monitor children and adolescents at risk. Medication, supportive therapy, and family counselling can help to enhance the quality of life for children and families and permit youngsters to proceed with their development in the best possible way (Kaplan and Shachter, 1993).

B. DEPRESSION AND SUICIDAL BEHAVIOR. Just as with bipolar disorder, genetic predisposition appears to render some individuals vulnerable to major depression (Rauch et al., 1991), even though developmental and environmental factors play a critical role. And as with bipolar disorder some depressed adolescents may be diagnosed with borderline personality disorder (Wenning, 1990), while others conceal their depression by use of drugs, antisocial or delinquent behavior, running away, and hostility to adults (Meeks and Bernet, 1990; Bemporad and Lee, 1988). Often, however, the depression of adolescence resembles that of adulthood and may even surpass it in terms of depth of despair. As Bemporad and Lee (1988) point out, adolescents have not attained the moderation in thinking and action that comes with life experience and "the repeated getting over losses, humiliations, and frustrations that normally occur in the course of growing up" (p. 641). Rather, they manifest an all-or-nothing approach to themselves and the world. Accordingly, if they feel depressed they may believe they are totally worthless or failures forever, and their self-esteem may collapse. This is especially a possibility if adolescents have had earlier difficulties in achievement or peer relationships and are socially isolated.

Because of the propensity on the part of adolescents towards action, depressed adolescents must always be considered at risk for suicide. This is especially true when the depression is severe and when they are experiencing chronic and severe environmental stresses, especially family disintegration (Meeks and Bernet, 1990; Pfeffer, 1988). Any suicidal idea or action by an adolescent must be taken seriously, especially when the youngster writes a suicide note. Unfortunately, such suicidal ideas and actions are sometimes dismissed by parents and other adults as "bids for attention" or "gestures," and the teen fails to receive appropriate help.

Whenever adolescents have expressed suicidal ideas, have made suicidal attempts, or appear excessively preoccupied with death and fantasies of death, suicide must be discussed directly with them. Contrary to a commonly-held belief, discussion of suicide is *not* more likely to cause a person to commit suicide. Rather, individuals who signal their despair and are ignored are at increased risk. Examples of questions that can be asked are: Have you ever felt so bad that you wanted to kill yourself? Did you ever try to kill or injure yourself? Did you ever hurt yourself purposely or try to commit suicide? Before an adolescent gains trust in an adult, he or she may deny being suicidal and may behave in a guarded manner. However, the adult should persist in discussion of the issue, so that the young person may be more able to discuss suicidal tendencies (Pfeffer, 1988).

II. Schizophrenia

Schizophrenic psychosis often makes its first appearance during adolescence. As in the case of bipolar disorder, biological markers do not exist for the prediction of schizophrenia, but there does seem to be a genetic predisposition. Few researchers believe that psychogenic factors, such as abnormal family communication patterns, are in themselves causative. Rather, research appears to point to the probability that vulnerability to developing schizophrenia is based upon the interaction of genetic with environmental factors. A number of studies indicate that, as very young children, individuals who become schizophrenic show a variety of neurophysiological deficits and developmental dysfunctions (Kron and Kestenbaum, 1988).

The "negative" symptoms of schizophrenia (including social withdrawal and blunting of affect) often develop insidiously over a period of time and seem to cause little distress. Such a slow process usually indicates a chronic course of the illness that tends to be less responsive to treatment. On the other hand, the "positive" symptoms of schizophrenia (including delusions, hallucinations, and confusion) may develop rapidly and with accompanying anxiety. These "positive" symptoms are often more responsive to treatment, and may have a successful outcome if the young person has had a reasonable premorbid adjustment (Meeks and Bernet, 1990).

Despite the importance of early diagnosis and treatment for the optimal long term functioning of a young person with schizophrenia, the illness may prove difficult to identify in adolescence. A number of factors may be involved in this phenomenon. For one thing, adolescents with schizophrenia may try to present themselves as "typical teenagers with problems," including drug abuse, and may be mistaken for such teens. In other cases, youngsters who present behavioral problems or who are involved in delinquent activities may actually prove to be schizophrenic. Then, too, many adults are reluctant to recognize that such a grave and potentially debilitating illness may be present in a teenager (Meeks and Bernet, 1990). However, appropriate treatment and realistic long-term planning for a schizophrenic adolescent can lead the way toward a more successful future.

ADOLESCENT VICTIMS

It is well known that physical and sexual abuse correlates with an increased risk of delinquency and violence in adolescence. In addition, recent research now indicates that physical neglect by itself (defined as severe lack of food, clothing, shelter, and medical attention) may also have a serious impact in adolescence (Widom, 1991). Both abused and neglected youngsters have a greater incidence of delinquency, and abused or neglected adolescent girls show a higher incidence of juvenile offenses involving violence than girls who did not experience abuse or neglect. Even when adolescents do not act out following a history of abuse or neglect, more subtle manifestations of emotional difficulty may be present, including depression, emotional withdrawal, or suicidal behavior (Widom, 1991).

In recent years the devastating impact of sexual abuse (especially incest) has begun to be better understood, and professionals working with adolescents are advised to look for it in a variety of problem situations (Forward, 1988; Kempe and Kempe, 1984; Goodwin, 1982). For example, hospitalized psychiatric patients, including those diagnosed as borderline, show an elevated incidence of sexual abuse and physical abuse in their histories (Meeks and Bernet, 1990; Green, 1988). In addition, depersonalization, dissociation and multiple personalities may be seen in individuals who have experienced incest or childhood sexual abuse (Meeks and Bernet, 1990). A childhood history of sexual abuse has also been noted in individuals who became prostitutes, substance abusers, and addicts or developed sexual difficulties, depression, sleep disturbances, anxiety, promiscuity, and self-destructive thoughts (Green, 1988). Young people who have been victims of incest also have an increased risk of becoming victims of crimes (including rape) and violence (Green, 1988).

Pagelow (1984) has pointed out the correlation between runaway behavior and abuse, especially sexual abuse. Many runaways "are not running *toward* something, but rather are running *away* from something..." (p. 49) Indeed, for some youngsters running away may actually represent adaptive behavior (Widom, 1991). Thus, when an adolescent has run away, especially if the runaway is associated with promiscuity or prostitution, it is extremely important to check for the presence of abuse in the home.

When an adolescent is the victim of a trauma, he or she may develop the symptoms of Post-Traumatic Stress Disorder (DSM-IV, 1994). These symptoms include repetitive and intrusive recollections, recurrent distressing dreams, flashbacks, avoidance of stimuli associated with the trauma, sleep disturbances, irritability and hypervigilance. Some researchers have suggested that there needs to be an additional diagnostic formulation for individuals who have been victims of repeated, prolonged trauma. Herman (1992) presents the criteria for Complex Post-Traumatic Stress Disorder, which would apply to those who have suffered childhood physical or sexual abuse, along with other victims such as hostages, concentration camp survivors, religious cult survivors, and survivors of organized sexual exploitation. Some of the symptoms of Complex Post-Traumatic Stress Disorder are, in addition to those noted above, shame, guilt and self blame; sense of stigma; preoccupation with the perpetrator; alteration of relations with others; and sense of despair (Herman, 1992).

LEARNING DISABILITIES AND ATTENTION DEFICIT HYPERACTIVITY DISORDER

According to the Centers for Disease Control, learning disabilities

(LD) affect between 5 percent and 10 percent of children (Silver, 1989). These neurologically based disorders frequently occur in tandem with attention deficit hyperactivity disorder (ADHD), which is also neurologically based. Learning-disabled children are often inattentive, although it is not always clear whether this represents withdrawal from difficult tasks, the presence of an attention deficit disorder, or something else (Jansky, 1988).

LD and ADHD are lifelong conditions and may impact social functioning as well as school performance. Research has shown that children and adolescents with LD are at greater risk of depression from profound and constant feelings of failure. Such depression in learning disabled adolescents increases the risk of suicide (Jansky, 1988). Some researchers have suggested that children with LD are more prone to emotional problems not merely as a secondary reaction to school failure but as a direct result of cognitive difficulties that, in turn, affect social relations and self-esteem (Kronick, 1981; Rosenberger, 1988).

Weiss and her colleagues (1985) followed children with ADHD into adulthood. Their research showed that in adolescence more than half of the young people were displaying significant or very serious problems, including problems with work, intimate relationships, and impulsive behavior. A small but significant number were either severely psychiatrically disturbed (as manifested by admissions to psychiatric hospitals, few friends or even acquaintances, and serious depressions including suicide attempts) or displaying antisocial behavior (unemployment, jail terms). Other researchers have found that individuals with neurologically based disorders like ADHD and LD have an increased risk of substance abuse, delinquency, and serious emotional difficulties including psychiatric hospitalization (Kaplan and Shachter, 1991; Wender et al., 1981). Johnson (1988) has pointed out that such individuals display characteristics that typify the Borderline Personality, including "impulsivity, irritability, poor frustration tolerance, aggressive outbursts and temper tantrums, readiness to anger, drug and alcohol abuse, suicidal gestures...[and] mood swings..." (p. 253).

It is often assumed that children with LD and ADHD will be identified in the early grades and given remediation at that point in their school career. While this is frequently the case, a surprising number do not come to the attention of educational and other specialists until adolescence, and some individuals go through school without their problems being identified at all (Kaplan and Shachter,

1991). Adolescents with early-identified LD and ADHD have had the advantage of academic supports and, where appropriate, medication to improve concentration and reduce impulsivity. In optimal circumstances they are taught to compensate for their disabilities so that they can feel more successful in school and in their social relationships.

When youngsters with LD or ADHD reach adolescence without having received any assistance, they may experience academic, social, emotional, or behavioral difficulties. Because the nature of the problem is not understood, the teen may be suffering from low self-esteem and self-blame, and the family and school may regard him or her as an underachiever or a troublemaker. Adolescence represents, for many individuals, a last chance for educational and therapeutic intervention. Poorly understood problems will be inadequately treated. On the other hand, educational remediation, appropriate medication, and/or supportive therapy offers young people a chance to make a more satisfactory life adjustment.

CONCLUSION

Drawing upon established theories as well as recent research, this chapter has presented an overview of the developmental processes of childhood and adolescence as they impact upon adolescent outcomes. These outcomes may be either relatively adaptive or dysfunctional, depending upon factors of risk, vulnerability, and resilience in the individual, the environment, or both. Specific problems of adolescence have also been examined, and the relationship between adolescent substance abuse and risk and vulnerability has been highlighted within an ecosystemic framework.

Adolescence is a crucial transition, containing both possibilities and perils. Adults frequently respond to adolescents with apprehension. Young people, for their part, may confuse adults because of their tendency to act out negatively, in what Meeks and Bernet (1990) have termed "misdirection." Yet adolescents continue to need adult support and guidance. The greater the understanding provided by the concerned adult, the better the chance that the young person's adaptation will be strengthened. When adolescent substance abuse is placed in the context of both developmental issues and specific disorders, interventions will be enhanced.

REFERENCES

Aichhorn, A. (1963). *Wayward Youth*. New York: Viking Press.

Akiskal, H. (1989). New insights into the nature and heterogeneity of mood disorders. *Journal of Clinical Psychiatry, 50*(supplement), 6-10.

Anthony, E., and Scott, P. (1960). Manic depressive psychosis in childhood. *Journal of Child Psychology and Psychiatry, 1,* 53-72.

Arnold, L. (Ed.), (1990). *Childhood Stress*. New York: John Wiley and Sons.

Bemporad, J., and Lee, K. (1988). Affective disorders. In C. Kestenbaum and D. Williams (Eds.), *Handbook of Clinical Assessment of Children and Adolescents*, pp. 626-649. New York: NYU Press.

Blos, P. (1979). *The Adolescent Passage*. New York: International Universities Press.

Blos, P. (1962). *On Adolescence*. New York: Free Press.

Bowlby, J. (1982). *Attachment*. Second Edition. New York: Basic Books.

Bowlby, J. (1973). *Separation: Anxiety and Anger*. New York: Basic Books.

Bowlby, J. (1980). *Loss: Sadness and Depression*. New York: Basic Books.

Brooks-Gunn, J. (1991). How stressful is the transition to adolescence for girls? In M. Colten and S. Gore (Eds.), *Adolescent Stress: Causes and Consequences,* pp. 131-149. New York: Aldine.

Dornbusch, S., Mont-Reynaud, R., Ritter, P., Chen, Zeng-yin, and Steinberg, L. (1991). Stressful events and their correlates among adolescents of diverse backgrounds. In M. Colten and S. Gore (Eds.), *Adolescent Stress: Causes and Consequences,* pp.111-130. New York: Aldine.

DSM-IV: Diagnostic and Statistical Manual of Mental Disorders. (1994). Fourth Edition. Washington, D.C.: American Psychiatric Association.

Eisen, P. (1972). The infantile roots of adolescent violence. *American Journal of Psychoanalysis,* 36(3), 211-218.

Erikson, E. (1950). *Childhood and Society.* New York: Norton.

Erikson, E. (1968). *Identity: Youth and Crisis.* New York: Norton.

Flavell, J. (1963). *The Developmental Psychology of Jean Piaget.* New York: Van Nostrand.

Forward, S. (1988). *Betrayal of Innocence: Incest and Its Devastation.* New York: Penguin Books.

Freud, A. (1958). Adolescence. *Psychoanalytic Study of the Child,* 13, 255-278. New York: International Universities Press.

Freud, A. (1967). Comments on trauma. In S. Furst (Ed.), *Psychic Trauma,* pp.235-245. New York: Basic Books.

Garmezy, N. (1991). Resiliency and vulnerability to adverse developmental outcomes associated with poverty. *The American Behavioral Scientist,* 34(4), 416-430.

Gibbs, J., Huang, L., and Associates. (1989). *Children of Color: Psychological Interventions with Minority Youth.* San Francisco: Jossey-Bass.

Gilligan, C., Lyons, N., and Hanmer, T. (Eds.). (1990). *Making Connections: The Relational Worlds of Adolescent Girls at Emma Willard School.* Cambridge, MA: Harvard University Press.

Goodman, J. (1988). The court-referred aggressive child and adolescent. In C. Kestenbaum and D. Williams (Eds.), *Handbook of Clinical Assessment of Children and Adolescents,* pp.1006-1023. New York: NYU Press.

Goodwin, J. (1982). *Sexual Abuse: Incest Victims and their Families.* Boston: John Wright.

Green, A., (1988). The abused child and adolescent. In C. Kestenbaum and D. Williams (Eds.), *Handbook of Clinical Assessment of Children and Adolescents,* pp. 842-863. New York: NYU Press.

Hauser, S., Powers, S., and Noam, G. (1991). *Adolescents and Their Families: Paths of Ego Development.* New York: Free Press.

Herman, J. (1992). *Trauma and Recovery.* New York: Basic Books.

Inclan, J., and Herron, D. (1989). Puerto Rican adolescents. In *Children of Color: Psychological Interventions with Minority Youth,* Gibbs, J., Huang, L., and Associates (Eds.), pp. 251-277. San Francisco: Jossey Bass.

Jansky, J. (1988). Assessment of learning disabilities. In C. Kestenbaum and D. Williams (Eds.), *Handbook of Clinical Assessment of Children and Adolescents,* pp. 296-311. New York: NYU Press.

Johnson, H. (1988). Where is the border? Current issues in the diagnosis and treatment of the borderline. *Clinical Social Work Journal,* 16, 243-260.

Kaplan, C., and Shachter, E. (1991). Adults with undiagnosed learning disabilities: practice considerations. *Families in Society,* 74(4), 195-201.

Kaplan, C., and Shachter, E. (1993). Diagnostic and treatment issues with childhood bipolar disorders. *Clinical Social Work Journal,* 21(3), 271-281.

Kaplan, L. (1984). *Adolescence: The Farewell to Childhood.* New York: Simon and Schuster.

Kempe, R., and Kempe, C. (1984). *The Common Secret: Sexual Abuse of Children and Adolescents.* New York: Freeman.

Kron, L., and Kestenbaum, C. (1988). Children at risk for psychotic disorder in adult life. In C. Kestenbaum and D. Williams (Eds.), *Handbook of Clinical Assessment of Children and Adolescents,* pp. 650-672. New York: NYU Press.

Kronick, D. (1981). *Social Development of Learning Disabled Persons.* San Francisco: Jossey-Bass.

Larson, R. and Asmussen, L. (1991). Anger, worry and hurt in early adolescence: an enlarging world of negative emotions. In M. Colton and S. Gore (Eds.) *Adolescent Stress: Causes and Consequences,* pp. 21-41. New York: Aldine.

Laufer, M. (1966). Object loss and mourning during adolescence. *Psychoanalytic Study of the Child,* 2, pp. 269-293. New York: International Universities Press.

Mahler, M., Pine, F., and Bergman, A. (1975). *Psychological Birth of the Human Infant—Symbiosis and Individuation.* New York: Basic Books.

Marohn, R., Locke, E., Rosenthal, R., and Curtis, G. (1982). Juvenile delinquency and violent deaths. In S. Feinstein, J. Looney, S. Schwartzberg and A. Sorosky (Eds.), *Adolescent Psychiatry, Vol. 10, Developmental and Clinical Studies,* pp.147-170.

Masterson, J. (1967). The symptomatic adolescent five years later: he didn't grow out of it. *American Journal of Psychiatry,* 123, 1388-1345.

Masterson, J. (1968). The psychiatric significance of adolescent turmoil. *American Journal of Psychiatry,* 124, 1549-1554.

Meeks, J., and Bernet, W. (1990). *The Fragile Alliance.* Malabar, Florida: Krieger Publishing Co.

Miller, D. (1983). *The Age Between.* Northvale, NJ: Jason Aronson.

Mishne, J. (1986). *Clinical Work with Adolescents.* New York: Free Press.

Myers, H., and King, L. (1983). Mental health issues in the development of black American children. In G. Powell, J. Yamamoto, A. Romero and A. Morales (Eds.), *The Psychosocial Development of Minority Group Children,* pp. 275-306. New York: Brunner Mazel.

Offer, D. (1969). *The Psychological World of the Teenager.* New York: Basic Books.

Offer, D. (1987). The mystery of adolescence. *Adolescent Psychiatry,* 14, 7-27.

Pagelow, M. (1984). *Family Violence.* New York: Praeger.

Petersen, A., Kennedy, R., and Sullivan, P. (1991). Coping with adolescence. In *Adolescent Stress: Causes and Consequences,* M. Colton and S. Gore (Eds.), pp. 93-110. New York: Aldine.

Pfeffer, C. (1988). Child and adolescent suicide risk. In C. Kestenbaum and D. Williams (Eds.), *Handbook of Clinical Assessment of Children and Adolescents,* pp. 673-688. New York: NYU Press.

Piaget, J. (1967). *Six Psychological Studies.* New York: Random House.

Rauch, J., Sarno, C., and Simpson, S. (1991). Screening for affective disorders. *Families in Society,* 72, 602-609.

Rosenberger, J. (1988). Self psychology as a theoretical base for understanding the impact of learning disabilities. *Child and Adolescent Social Work Journal,* 5, 269-280.

Rutter, M. (1987). Psychosocial resilience and protective mechanisms. *American Journal of Orthopsychiatry,* 57(3), 316-331.

Sarnoff, C. (1976). *Latency*. New York: Jason Aronson.

Schlegel, A., and Barry, H. (1991). *Adolescence: An Anthropological Inquiry*. New York: Free Press.

Schmidt, K., and Friedson, S. (1990). Atypical outcome in attention deficit hyperactivity disorder. *Journal of the American Academy of Child and Adolescent Psychiatry*, 29, 566-569.

Silver, L. (1989). Learning disabilities: Introduction. *Journal of the American Academy of Child and Adolescent Psychiatry*, 28, 309-313.

Simmons, R., Burgeson, R., Carleton-Ford, S., and Blyth, D. (1987). The impact of cumulative change in early adolescence. *Child Development*, 58, 1220-1238.

Spitz, R. (1965). *The First Year of Life: A Psychoanalytic Study of Normal and Deviant Development of Object Relations*. New York: International Universities Press.

Turner, S., Norman, E., and Zunz, S. (1994). *From Risk to Resiliency, A Paradigm Shift: A Literature Review and Annotated Bibliography*. Unpublished manuscript. Fordham University.

Weiss, G., Hechtman, L., Milroy, T., and Perlman, T. (1985). Psychiatric status of hyperactives as adults: A controlled prospective 15 year follow-up of 63 hyperactive children. *Journal of the American Academy of Child Psychiatry*, 24, 211-220.

Wender, P., Reimherr, F., and Wood, D. (1981). Attention deficit disorder ("minimal brain dysfunction") in adults: A replication study of diagnosis and drug treatment. *Archives of General Psychiatry*, 38, 449-456.

Wenning, K. (1990). Borderline children: a closer look at diagnosis and treatment. *American Journal of Orthopsychiatry*, 60, 225-232.

Werner, E., and Smith, R. (1992). *Overcoming the Odds: High Risk Children from Birth to Adulthood*. Ithaca, NY: Cornell University Press.

Widom, C. (1991). Childhood victimization: risk factor for delinquency. In *Adolescent Stress: Causes and Consequences,* M. Colton and S. Gore (Eds.), pp. 201-221. New York: Aldine.

Winnicott, D. (1973). Delinquency as a sign of hope. In S. Feinstein and P. Giovacchini (Eds.), *Adolescent Psychiatry, Vol. 2, Developmental and Clinical Studies,* pp. 364-371. New York: Basic Books.

Zunz, S., Turner, S., and Norman, E. (1993). Accentuating the positive: Stressing resiliency in school-based substance abuse prevention programs. *Social Work in Education,* 15(3), 169-176.

CHAPTER 2

Prevention Programs Reviewed: What Works?

Elaine Norman, Sandra Turner, Sharyn J. Zunz, and Kathy Stillson

The use of legal and illegal substances such as tobacco, alcohol, and other drugs by youngsters continues to be a major concern in the United States and other countries. A recent survey conducted in New York State substantiates that concern. By high school graduation, 75 percent of the youngsters studied had used alcohol, 46 percent had used tobacco, 24 percent had used marijuana, and 6 percent had used cocaine (Bry and Krinsley, 1990). Such figures actually represent a downward trend from the late 1970s when adolescent substance use was much higher (U.S. Public Health Service, 1995). A small jump in marijuana and other illicit drug use among teenagers occurred in 1993 and 1994, the latest years for which such data is available. However, 1994 figures still remain lower than for most previous years (Swan, 1995).

A number of suggestions can be made to explain the reasons for the downturn over the past fifteen or twenty years in adolescent substance use. Some of the explanations include: the fad quality of taking drugs has worn off; their symbolic value as a form of rebellion has decreased; adolescents have been affected by the general movement in this country toward more healthy lifestyles; political and professional leaders have taken a stand against using drugs; and parents, schools, communities, and media have become more sophisticated in their message about, and their programs concerning, the non-use of such substances.

It is the last explanation, the anti-use messages and programs that are the focus of this chapter. The chapter will detail the components of the major school-based curriculum-type prevention programs utilized in the past twenty years and report on the results of research evaluations of each strategy. A short review will be provided of the theories of human behavior upon which each of the major prevention strategies is based. Additionally, a list is given of many of the *successful* programs and sources of curriculum materials and training in program use. However, first it is important to mention a few points concerning adolescent substance use and abuse and the programs we will be discussing.

EXPERIMENTATION AND USE—MEANINGFUL FUNCTIONS

Alcohol and other drug use among youth ranges from simple experimentation, which could be considered as normal behavior, to abuse, which is obviously dysfunctional behavior. It is important to consider the possibility that some substance use can serve meaningful purposes in an adolescent's life. One study that looked at the differences between abstainers, experimenters, and frequent users of substances found that youngsters who experimented with alcohol and other drugs (mainly marijuana) but were not frequent users were the best adjusted of all study subjects. The youngsters with the most anxious and restricted personalities and the poorest social skills were the ones who had not experimented at all by age eighteen. The frequent users were found to be maladjusted and alienated and had poor impulse control and emotional distress (Shedler and Block, 1990).

According to Jessor (1985) substance use can serve important functions in adolescents' lives, such as expressing opposition to authority, affirming solidarity with peers, coping with feelings of inadequacy, marking transitions from immaturity, and relieving feelings of boredom and loneliness. However, experimentation is often illegal (depending on age and substance,) and can cross over into harmful frequent use.

The evaluated prevention programs reported on in this chapter have targeted abstainers and experimenters with the aim of preventing future serious use. Frequent users have rarely been participants in such programs.

AGE OF FIRST USE

There is general agreement that the longer one can delay the age of first use of substances, the greater the likelihood that abuse will be prevented. With advancing age youngsters develop greater coping, social, and resistance skills, and become aware of more options and have more interests. The longer first use is delayed, the more personal resources are brought to bear to prevent future abuse. A study by Jessor (1985) supports that conclusion. Fifty percent of males who initiated drug use before the age of fifteen later developed a substance abuse problem. Among those who initiated use between the ages of fifteen and seventeen, 26 percent went on to develop a problem; for those who initiated use between eighteen and twenty-four, 17 percent later developed a problem; of the first time initiators 25 years or older, only 11 percent eventually developed an abuse problem.

Although there is general agreement about the significance of delaying the age of first use, there is no consensus about when to begin prevention efforts. Some in the field feel that prevention efforts should be started as early as possible—even in kindergarten or the first grade. Others feel that it is a waste of resources to start that early—that it is best to start when youth are under pressure from social and environmental stressors (Johnson, 1982). This is most likely to occur about age twelve. In fact, ages twelve through fifteen are particularly vulnerable. The physical changes of puberty, the change of schools from elementary to junior high, the intense pressure to conform with peers, and the budding desire to be independent from parents and authority all add to the vulnerability of that age. The easy availability of substances and the knowledge that they may temporarily relieve the psychological pain and turmoil of adolescence confront youngsters with choices that they may not be capable of making constructively.

In the 1970s, when adolescent prevention efforts were just beginning, high schools were targeted as the appropriate intervention point. By the late 1970s, the realization that younger children should be targeted dominated, and junior high schools and primary schools were targeted for prevention programs. Today, a large number of programs start in the sixth or seventh grades. Many experts still argue that starting at an even earlier grade is beneficial and thus start some prevention programs as early as kindergarten. The programs of the 1980s, which form the focus of this chapter, targeted sixth and seventh grades primarily.

PRIMARY, SECONDARY, AND TERTIARY PREVENTION

Prevention efforts take place on three levels. Primary prevention refers to strategies that aim to influence everyone to *abstain* from any form of substance use. Secondary prevention encompasses efforts to keep social/recreational experimenters from becoming regular or heavy users. Tertiary prevention is aimed at youth already engaged in serious drug-taking. It usually represents some form of treatment for those who already have a problem with substances to prevent the problem from getting worse or having a "domino effect" in other areas of life.

Primary and secondary efforts will be the focus of the rest of this chapter. Tertiary prevention efforts are not examined.

THE PROGRAMS

Four major strategies have been employed in the search for an effective substance abuse prevention model (Silverman, 1988). Three of them, the Information Only, the Alternative Activities, and the Competency Enhancement strategies, when delivered alone, have proven to be either not at all or negligibly effective. The fourth, the Social Environmental strategy, which is a combination of parts of the first three plus much more, has had very encouraging results.

What follows is a review of the dozens of scientifically designed research evaluations of the effectiveness of the four prevention strategies undertaken in the last decade or so. Those studies suggest what activities help to prevent substance abuse and what activities do not. The research is primarily about *school-based* prevention programs. (The following chapter in this book by Sharyn J. Zunz reports on community-based prevention programs.) The substances addressed include tobacco, alcohol, marijuana, and other drugs.

The Information Only Program Strategy

The aim of Information Only programs, which flourished in the 1960s and 1970s but are still quite numerous today, was to reduce use by educating youngsters in classrooms about substances.

Information was offered about:
* the properties of particular drugs;
* potential physical reactions to particular drugs;
* methods of use; and
* the short-term and long-term social and health consequences of use.

A sub-set of programs used scare tactics:
* dramatizing the negative aspects of use;
* exaggerating harmful effects; and
* addressing only adverse consequences.

The model assumed that youngsters had not previously learned about the dangers and adverse consequences of using drugs. By filling in that gap and supplying information, it was expected that youngsters would thereafter make appropriate choices *not* to use drugs. Such thinking is most closely aligned with Cognitive and Social Inoculation Theory (McGuire, 1968; Evans et al., 1981). Both theories posit that adolescents can be protected against the pressures to begin alcohol and other drug use. This can be seen to be very much like receiving a vaccine or an inoculation. Information Only programs were based on the idea that providing information about certain substances and the dangers of their use would serve as a protective "vaccine," immunizing youngsters against the pressures to use that young people are likely to face.

Unfortunately, the accumulated research clearly indicates that the theory and the programs had negligible and sometimes even counter-productive results (Moskowitz et al., 1984b). In their review of 127 prevention programs, Schaps et al. (1981) found Information Only strategies produced the worst outcome ratings. Tobler's (1986) meta-analysis found such programs to have little or no effect on attitudes, skills, use of drugs, or other behavior. Bruvold and Rundall's (1988) meta-analysis also found Information Only programs, which they called "the rational approach," to be the most ineffective of all studied program types in changing substance-use behavior.

Some researchers have attempted to explain why this program type has had such disappointing outcomes. The most convincing explanation was suggested by Weisheit (1983) who did not believe that a few hours of classroom instruction about the dangers of substances could possibly supersede years of learning about the worthiness and acceptability of cigarettes, alcohol, and marijuana from parents, peers, and media. Hawkins and his colleagues (Hawkins et al., 1985) suggest that the exaggerated negative claims made in some of these programs tended to be disbelieved by many young people, and this undermined their confidence in the entire program. In some cases, the information supplied actually aroused curiosity and increased initial experimentation by the young people. Finally, youngsters do have the tendency to ignore their own physical vulnerability and potential mortality and to believe that the adverse consequences "would not happen to me."

Whatever the reasons, Information Only programs do not impact substance use very effectively. They do, however, impact knowledge acquisition (Tobler, 1986; Hansen et al., 1988b). Since that is seen as a prerequisite to abstinence, information components, especially the *short-term immediate* social and health consequences of use, have been included in other prevention strategies.

The Alternative Activities Program Strategy

By involving youth in absorbing and satisfying non-drug-related activities, the Alternative Activities strategy was intended to reduce and/or prevent substance use. Recreational programs and special projects offered youth the ability to assume responsible roles, to relieve boredom, to increase self-esteem, and, most importantly, to bond to community values. The approach emphasized providing youthful involvement in a positive environment with the opportunity for fulfilling experiences. The non-use of substances was *not* a primary focus of such programs since it was assumed that participating in the activities themselves would be enough to counteract any tendency to initiate alcohol and other drug use. It is highly likely that that omission contributed greatly to the *ineffectiveness* of most Alternative Activities programs.

The theoretical foundation for this strategy was Social Learning Theory, initially conceptualized by Bandura (1977). This theory posits that behavior is learned by observing and then imitating the behavior of other people (especially one's parents and other role models,) as well as by being alert to the reactions of significant others to one's own behavior (Kim, 1988). Importance is placed on an individual's self-regulating capacities. Youngsters have the capacity to anticipate the consequences of their own behavior. They are able to exercise control over that behavior within the confines of their environment. Young people who do well at various tasks offered in an Alternatives program will most likely be reacted to positively by peers, family members, and teachers. This positive response will be internalized, enhancing individuals' positive bonding to school, family, and community values (Rhodes and Jason, 1987).

A large share of prevention resources have been spent on Alternatives programs even though most published reports document their ineffectiveness. The California "NAPA" project implemented two Alternatives programs with junior high school students, a cross-age tutoring program, and the operation of a school store. Both failed to produce positive substance use outcomes (Schaps et al., 1986; Moskowitz et al., 1983, 1984a). The "Channel One" program that involved youth in business projects proved to be counter productive, resulting in increased use of substances and increased frequency of drunkenness (Stein et al., 1984). The school-based "Positive Alternatives for Youth" program that included physical and creative-expressive activities did show lower hard liquor use, especially among those students with the greatest involvement in the activities. But by the two-year follow-up, this positive result no longer existed (Cook et al., 1984).

Some evidence suggests that the type of activity in the program might affect the outcome. Swisher and Hu (1983) suggest that social activities, with substance users present, such as sports, entertainment, vocational, and extra-curricular activities, are associated with increased use. More solitary activities like hobbies, academic preparation, and religious activities are associated with decreased use.

Macro reviews give a somewhat less negative picture of this strategy. In their review of 127 prevention programs, Schaps et al. (1981) included twelve Alternatives programs. Five showed positive results, while seven showed no impact. One meta-analysis suggested that Alternatives programs with skills acquisition components and a large number of hours of programming could be effective with "high-risk" youth (Tobler, 1986).

In general, the preponderance of negative outcomes have influenced professionals in the field to almost entirely discount the Alternatives strategy as effective in substance use prevention. One group has made the following strong statement: "Alternatives programs as currently conceived and implemented are likely to be ineffective as prevention measures" (Schaps et al., 1986).

Weisheit (1983) explains the continued popularity of both Information Only and Alternative Activities programs in the face of research results documenting their ineffectiveness as probably due to the larger social and political context in which they have arisen. There is a public demand "that something be done," and prevention programs, even those with such doubtful impact as the two we have just discussed, at least meet the public's demand for action.

The Competency Enhancement Program Strategy

This program strategy assumes that youngsters use drugs because they have low self-esteem, inappropriate values, and inadequate decision-making, problem-solving, and/or communication skills. By enhancing the personal and social competency of youngsters through specialized skills training in those areas, substance use will be reduced. Programs utilizing this strategy engage in the following activities:

* Self-concept building;
* Stress management and stress reduction techniques;
* Rational decision making;
* Problem solving;
* Assertiveness training;
* Communication enhancement; and
* Values examination.

The theoretical foundation for this strategy is Problem Behavior Theory (Jessor and Jessor, 1977). The theory contends that early dysfunctional behavior is associated with drug use and abuse. Antisocial behavior of young children (such as being both aggressive and shy) can interfere with making friends and developing a sense of belonging to a school and community. This can be the early sign of later maladaptive behavior such as substance abuse. Environments that contribute to "problem behavior" are homes and school where boundaries and roles are not clearly defined. Parents who have close relationships with their children and who are involved in a positive way in their activities help mitigate against problem behavior.

Youngsters who are the most likely to initiate regular use and abuse of drugs are those alienated from the dominant values of their school and community, who have a high tolerance for deviant behavior and normlessness as well as resistance to traditional authority, who are sensation seeking and show little concern for safety, who perform poorly in school, and who associate with peers who use drugs (Hawkins et al., 1985).

Competency Enhancement programs typically target general goals rather than specifically targeting substance-use prevention (Hansen, 1988a). They aim to enhance personal and social competency by teaching broad coping skills. Also, the *non-use* of substances is not specifically focused upon in the programming. Possibly those two facts explain why, as with the two strategies previously discussed, the evaluations of these programs have not shown the effectiveness of this strategy in preventing or decreasing substance use.

Of the 127 programs Schaps et al. (1981) studied, sixty were of this type. Thirty-seven of the sixty showed *no* effect on drug-specific outcomes, twenty showed a small positive effect, and only three a noteworthy positive effect.

Because of its widespread use, the "Here's Looking at You" program modeled in this vein is worth describing in detail. This program targeted alcohol use specifically. It was designed to increase knowledge about alcohol as a pharmacological agent and alcoholism as a social problem, to enhance self-esteem, to instill appropriate attitudes favoring either abstinence or moderate use, and to teach decision-making skills to assist youth in making responsible decisions about the use of alcohol. The program was extensively implemented in grades K through 12 nationally. Designed for fifteen classroom periods per school year in each grade, huge amounts were spent on the implementation and the evaluation of this curriculum. The available evidence indicates that the strategy, and its revision "Here's Looking at You, Two," was ineffective. Although there was attitudinal gain, the program did not impact on either the youngster's intentions about future use of alcohol nor actual drinking behavior. Cigarette and other drug use was also measured even though only alcohol was a specific target of the program. There was no carryover effect of the program on those substances either (Hopkins et al., 1988; Kim, 1988).

Finally, Tobler's (1986) meta-analysis of prevention programs corroborated the negative reviews for this Competency Enhancement strategy, leading her to state that "solid evidence exists for discontinuing their use."

Despite discouraging reviews, the three strategies just discussed have not been completely abandoned. Elements of each have been blended into programs based on the Social Environmental strategy (which will be discussed next) with very promising results.

The Social Environmental Strategy

In the Social Environmental strategy the aim is to reduce substance use by supplying youngsters with motivation and resistance skills. Initially this strategy was referred to as the Social Learning model and was thus confused with the theory of the same name, which formed only part of the underpinnings of the program type.

Social Learning Theory, Cognitive or Social Inoculation Theory, and Biopsychosocial Theory all contribute to the foundation of this program type. As was previously mentioned, the first theory stresses imitation and modeling; the second, the inhibition of unwanted behaviors. The third theory emphasizes the influence of family, school, and community upon youngsters, highlighting the importance of the interaction between persons and their internal and external environments. (Wills and Shiffman, 1985; Hawkins and Weiss, 1985; Kumpfer and DeMarsh, 1985; Kumpfer and Turner, 1990). The new name, the Social Environmental strategy, is more expressive of the multiple theoretical frameworks upon which the model is based.

The late 1980s and early 1990s witnessed the accumulation of sufficient evidence to indicate that programs utilizing the Social Environmental strategy are consistently (although modestly) effective in reducing the use of substances.

The strategy assumes that social influences from peers, parents, and media encourage substance use. Youngsters can be inoculated against those social pressures by reinforcing social norms against the use of substances and by supplying them with skills to resist social pressures to use. The components of this strategy include the following:

* Normative education with the goal of motivating the youngsters to abstain from substance use;
* Training in identifying pressures to use; and
* Training in resisting pressures to use.

The normative education component covers such things as an examination of the reasons young people use substances; an exploration, using participatory techniques, of misconceptions about the prevalence and acceptability of substances (e.g., "everyone" uses them); and the development within the classroom group of non-use norms and expectations, sometimes including public commitment statements by the participants not to use substances.

Participants are taught to identify social influences and pressure situations. They are made aware of the influences to use substances from peers, families, and the media. The forms peer pressure can take, discerning user-parent messages, and the critical analysis of media messages, are all included. Participants are also helped to recognize their own internal pressures to use.

Participants are taught specific skills with which to undermine such influences. Strategies are developed, modeled, role-played, repeated. Feedback and other reinforcement techniques are utilized to help participants achieve a sense of personal competence in executing each strategy.

A sizeable subset of successful programs of this kind also include components of the three strategies previously mentioned, adding, for example, information about the short-term social and personal consequences of use such as having a vehicle accident or acting out of control. Decision-making and problem-solving techniques, values clarification, stress management and self-worth enhancement activities are also often added (Botvin et al., 1983; Botvin and Eng, 1982; Pentz et al., 1989; Ellickson and Bell, 1990; Ellickson et al., 1993; MacKinnon et al., 1991).

Implementors

Teachers, school counselors, mental health professionals, and other prevention specialists have sometimes led Social Environmental programs sometimes with student peers. Peer implementors serve as role models and normative examples for the participants and therefore must be chosen with care. They have proven to be important contributors to successful program outcome (Leupker et al., 1983; Botvin et al., 1984; Murray et al., 1989; Perry et al., 1980; Schaps et al., 1981; Tobler, 1986). Student implementors are clearly not as skilled as professionals at classroom management or the facilitation of group discussion, and in order to be successful they need to be artfully chosen, adequately trained in program content and delivery, and eager to be involved in the activity (Botvin and Eng, 1982; Glynn, 1989).

Number of sessions

The number of classroom sessions actually included in the various programs has ranged from a low of four to a high of twenty. Sometimes the sessions are spread out over a school term or a school year. Sometimes they are concentrated into a few weeks. Studies isolating the optimal program length have not yet been done. One study compared weekly sessions with several-times-a-week sessions. The more intensive course proved to be the most effective (Botvin et al., 1983).

Participants

The population targeted in most prevention programs was white, middle-class youth. Many white, middle-class teenagers are at risk for using substances by virtue of genetic predisposition, or having parents who use substances, coming from dysfunctional families, doing poorly in school, having poor impulse control, and having poor social and coping skills. However, they do not face the same environmental stress from racism and poverty as inner-city minority youth.

A number of successful Social Environmental strategy prevention programs have targeted minorities. Gilchrist et al. (1987), and Schinke et al. (1988) offered successful programs to Native American adolescents. Hansen et al. (1988b) ran two programs with 75 percent minority participants and found resistance training to be successful. Newer programs have effectively targeted minority inner-city youth (Botvin et al., 1990).

Boosters

Results seem to be maintained from six months to two years before beginning to decay. By the fifth and sixth year after initial implementation, most results fade entirely (Flay et al., 1989; Murray et al., 1989). Booster sessions at periodic intervals after the initial program has been completed have been implemented by some programs to offset this decay. Ellickson and Bell (1990) consider them critical for maintaining effect. Botvin et al. (1983), Mathias (1994), and Perry et al. (1989) suggest that booster sessions can not only maintain effect, they can enhance it as well.

Parental involvement

Several successful school-based programs have included parents as part of their prevention package, utilizing the adults to help convey non-use messages and to enhance their youngsters' refusal skills. Biglan et al. (1987) used randomly selected parents to do the latter in their prevention program. Parental components of larger community prevention programs such as Project STAR and the Minnesota Smoking Prevention Program (see below) worked with parents to enhance their ability to convey non-use messages to their children.

Effectiveness for which substances?

The Social Environmental strategy seems to work better than any other tried to date. Positive results have been found with scores of programs of this type. The record is best for preventing tobacco use. The results for alcohol and other drugs are more limited but promising. Below are listed selected programs available to the public (usually for a fee) that have been shown to be successful in preventing use of tobacco only, alcohol only, and multiple substances. Contact persons and addresses, articles and research evaluations are listed for each program.

Name: Minnesota Smoking Prevention Program
References: (Luepker et al., 1983; Murray et al., 1989;
            Perry, 1987; Perry et al., 1989)
Address: Hazelden
            15251 Pleasant Valley Road
            P.O. Box 176
            Center City, MN 55012-0176
Contact   Safe and Drug Free Schools Coordinator
person: (800) 328-9000

Name: Project Path
            Refusal Skills Training and Parent messages in
            a Teacher Administered Program
Reference: (Biglan et al., 1987)
Address: Independent Video Devices
            401 E. 10th Ave #160
            Eugene, Oregon 97401
Contact
person: Bonnie Larson (503)345-3455

Name: Social Modeling Films to Deter Smoking in
            Adolescents: Houston Adolescent Smoking
            Project
Reference: (Evans et al., 1981)
Address: University of Houston
            Dept. of Psychology
            Central Campus
            Houston, Texas 77204-5341
Contact
person: Wanda Gaddis (713) 743-8556

Name:	Waterloo Smoking Prevention Project
References:	(Flay et al., 1985, 1989, 1990)
Address:	University of Waterloo,
	200 N. Ave 1, room MC 6082
	Waterloo, Ontario, Canada N2L 3G1
Contact	Steve Manske (519) 888-4747 or
person:	(519) 746-8171

SUCCESSFUL ALCOHOL (ONLY) PREVENTION PROGRAMS

Name:	Alcohol Education by the Teams-Games-
	Tournaments Method
Reference:	(Wodarski, 1987)
Address:	Dr. John Wodarski, Dir.
	University of Buffalo Research & Doctoral
	Program
	School of Social Work
	359 Baldy Hall, Box 601050
	Buffalo, New York 14260-1050
Contact	Dr. John Wodarski
person:	(716) 645-3381

Name:	Alcohol Misuse Prevention Study (AMPS)
References:	(Dielman et al., 1989; Shope et al., 1993)
Address:	Dr. T.E. Dielman
	Alcohol Misuse Prevention Study
	The University of Michigan Medical School
	G 1200 Towsley Center
	Box 0201
	Ann Arbor, Michigan 48109-0201
Contact	Lorraine Maxfield
person:	(513) 763-1154

Name: Inner City Youth Prevention Project
References: (Forgey and Schinke, in press; Forgey, 1994)
Address: Dr. Mary Ann Forgey
                   Fordham University at Lincoln Center
                   Graduate School of Social Service
                   113 West 60th Street
                   New York, New York 10023
Contact   Dr. Mary Ann Forgey
person: (212) 636-6654

SUCCESSFUL MULTIPLE SUBSTANCE PREVENTION PROGRAMS

Name: Adolescent Alcohol Prevention Trial AAPT
                   Project SMART
                   Tobacco and Alcohol Prevention Program
                   Project TAPP
References: (Hansen et al., 1988b; 1988c)
Address: University of Southern California
                   Institute for Prevention Research
                   1540 Alcazar Street CHP 207
                   Los Angeles, California 90033
Contact   Marny Barovich
person: (213) 342-2605

Name: Project ALERT
References: (Ellickson and Bell, 1990; Ellickson et al., 1993)
Address: Best Foundation for a Drug Free Tomorrow
                   13701 Riverside Drive, Suite 800
                   Sherman Oaks, California 91423
Contact   (800) 421-5055
number: (800) ALERT-10

Name: Life Skills Training (LST)
References: (Botvin et al., 1983; 1984; 1990; Dusenbury and Botvin, 1992)
Address: Princeton Health Press
414 Wall St.
Princeton, New Jersey 08540
Contact person: Steve Brod
(609) 921-0540

Name: Midwestern Prevention Project
Project STAR-Student Taught Awareness and Resistance
References: (Pentz et al., 1989; MacKinnon et al., 1991)
Address: Institute for Prevention Research
1540 Alcazar St., CHP 207
Los Angeles, California 90033
Contact person: Marny Barovich
(213) 342-2605

Name: Say It Straight
Reference: (Englander-Golden et al., 1986)
Address: Say It Straight Foundation
P.O. Box 50752
Denton, Texas 76206
Contact person: Dr. Paula Englander-Golden
(817) 383-4162

Name: SODAS Stop-Options-Decide-Act-Self Praise
Reference: (Schinke et al., 1988)
Address: Dr. Steven Schinke
Columbia University School of Social Work
622 West 113th Street
New York, New York 10025
Contact person: Dr. Steven Schinke
(212) 854-8506

CONCLUSION

After more than twenty-five years of planning, implementing, and evaluating curriculum-based substance abuse prevention programs for adolescents, a strategy has been developed which does seem to prevent or reduce the use of alcohol, tobacco and other illicit drugs. Two major components are essential factors in the programs' success: (1) the development of non-use norms and expectations among the teenagers, and (2) the training of those same teenagers to identify and to resist the social and situational pressures to use substances that they encounter on an almost daily basis. With this essential base, several other components have been added to successful programs such as information about the short-term social and personal consequences of use and specific competency enhancement techniques like stress management, decision-making and problem-solving strategies, self-esteem building and values clarification activities.

A sizable number of tested programs are available to the public. The "vaccine" to prevent adolescents from using tobacco, alcohol, and other drugs hasn't yet been found, but the Social Environmental program strategy described in this chapter offers encouraging results.

REFERENCES

Bandura, A. (1977). *Social Learning Theory.* Englewood Cliffs, NJ: Prentice Hall.

Biglan, A., Glasgow, R., Ary, D., Thompson, R., et al. (1987). How generalizable are the effects of smoking prevention programs? Refusal skills training and parent messages in a teacher administered program. *Journal of Behavioral Medicine, 10,* 613-628.

Botvin, G.J., and Eng, A. (1982). The efficacy of a multicomponent approach to the prevention of cigarette smoking. *Preventive Medicine, 11,* 199-211.

Botvin, G.J., Renick, N.L., and Baker, E. (1983). The effects of scheduling format and booster sessions on a broad spectrum psychosocial approach to smoking prevention. *Journal of Behavioral Medicine, 6(4),* 359-379.

Botvin, G.J., Baker, E., Botvin, E.M., Filazzola, A.D., et al. (1984). Prevention of alcohol misuse through the development of personal and social competence: A pilot study. *Journal Studies on Alcohol, 45,* 550-552.

Botvin, G.J., Baker, E., Dusenbury, L., Tortu, S., et al. (1990). Preventing adolescent drug abuse through a multimodel cognitive-behavioral approach: Results of a 3-year study. *Journal of Consulting and Clinical Psychology, 58(4),* 437-446.

Bruvold, W.H., and Rundall, T.G. (1988). A meta-analysis and theoretical review of school based tobacco and alcohol intervention programs. *Psychology and Health, 2,* 53-78.

Bry, B.H., and Krinsley, K.E. (1990). Adolescent substance abuse. In E. Feindler and G. Kalfus, (Eds.) *Adolescent Behavior Therapy Handbook,* pp. 275-302. New York: Springer Publishing.

Cook, R., Lawrence, H., Morse, C., and Roehl, J. (1984). An evaluation of the alternatives approach to drug abuse prevention. *International Journal of the Addictions, 19,* 767-787.

Dielman, T. E., Shope, J. T., Leech, S. L., and Butchart, A. T. (1989). Differential effectiveness of an elementary school-based alcohol misuse prevention program. *Journal of School Health, 59(6),* 255-263.

Dusenbury, L., and Botvin, G.J. (1992). Substance abuse prevention: Competence enhancement and the development of positive life options. *Journal of Addictive Diseases, 11(3),* 29-45.

Ellickson, P.L., and Bell, R.M. (1990). *Prospects for Preventing Drug Use Among Young Adolescents.* Santa Monica, CA: Rand Corporation.

Ellickson, P.L., Bell, R.M., and McGuigan, K. (1993). Preventing adolescent drug use: Long-term results of a junior high program. *American Journal of Public Health, 83(6),* 856-861.

Englander-Golden, P., Elconin, J., Miller, K.J., and Schwarzkopf, A. B. (1986). Brief "Say It Straight" training and follow-up in adolescent substance abuse prevention. *Journal of Primary Prevention, 6,* 219-230.

Evans, R., Rozelle, R., Maxwell, S., Raines, B., et al. (1981). Social modeling films to deter smoking in adolescents: Results of a three year field investigation. *Journal of Applied Psychology, 66,* 399-414.

Flay, B., Koepke, D., Thomson, S., and Santi, S., et al. (1989). Six year follow-up of the first Waterloo school smoking prevention trial. *American Journal of Public Health, 79(10),* 1371-1376.

Flay, B. R., Koepke, D., Thomson, S., Santi, S., et al. (1990). Six year follow-up of a school smoking prevention trial. *Brown University Digest of Addiction Theory and Applications,* 4-5.

Flay, B., Ryan, K., Best, J. A., Brown, K. S., et al. (1985). Are social-psychological smoking prevention programs effective? [The Waterloo Study]. *Journal of Behavioral Medicine, 8(1),* 37-59.

Forgey, M.A. (1994). Substance abuse prevention approaches for inner-city African-American and Hispanic youth. *Dissertation Abstracts International, 55(6),* (University Microfilms No. 9424069).

Forgey, M.A., and Schinke, S.P. (in press). School based interventions. In Wilson, D. K., Rodriguez, J. R., & Taylor, W. C. (Eds.), *Adolescent Health Promotion in Minority Populations.* Washington, D.C.: Health Psychology Division 38 American Psychology Association.

Gilchrist, L.D., Schinke, S.P., Trimble, J.E., and Cvetkovich, G. (1987). Skills enhancement to prevent substance abuse among American Indian adolescents. *International Journal of the Addictions, 22(9),* 869-879.

Glynn, T.J. (1989). Essential elements of school-based smoking prevention programs. *Journal of School Health, 59(5),* 171-188.

Hansen, W.B. (1988a). Effective school-based approaches to drug abuse prevention. *Educational Leadership, 45(6),* 9-14.

Hansen, W.B., Malotte, C., and Fielding, J. (1988b). Evaluation of a tobacco and alcohol abuse prevention curriculum for adolescents. *Health Education Quarterly, 15(1),* 93-114.

Hansen, W.B., Graham, J.W., Wolkenstein, B.H., and Rohrbach, L.A. (1988c). Effectiveness of fifth grade alcohol prevention programs of changing program-specific mediators of alcohol use [Paper presented at University of California, San Diego Conference "What Do We Know About School-Based Prevention Strategies: Alcohol, Tobacco and Other Drugs"]. San Diego, CA.

Hawkins, J.D., Lishner, D.M., Catalano, R.F., and Howard, M.O. (1985). Childhood predictors of adolescent substance abuse: Toward an empirically grounded theory. *Journal of Children in Contemporary Society, 18(1-2),* 11-48.

Hawkins, D., and Weiss, J.G. (1985). The social development model: An integrated approach to delinquency prevention. *Journal of Primary Prevention, 6(2),* 73-97.

Hopkins, R.H., Mauss, A.L., Kearney, A., and Weisheit, R.A. (1988). Comprehensive evaluation of a model alcohol education curriculum. *Journal of Studies on Alcohol, 49,* 38-50.

Jessor, R. (1985). Bridging etiology and prevention in drug abuse research. *N.I.D.A.-Research Monograph Series, 56,* 257-268.

Jessor, R., and Jessor, S. (1977). *Problem Behavior and Psychosocial Development.* New York: Academic Press.

Johnson, C.A. (1982). Untested and erroneous assumptions underlying antismoking programs. In T.J. Coates, A.C. Peterson and C. Perry (Eds.), *Promoting Adolescent Health: A Dialogue on Research and Practice,* pp. 149-165. New York: Academic Press.

Kim, S. (1988). A short- and long-term evaluation of "Here's Looking at You" alcohol education program. *Journal of Drug Education, 18(3),* 235-242.

Kumpfer, K., and DeMarsh, J. (1985). Family environmental and genetic influences on children's future chemical dependency. *Journal of Children in Contemporary Society, 18(1-2),* 49-91.

Kumpfer, K., and Turner, C. (1990). The social ecology model of adolescent substance abuse: Implications for prevention. *International Journal of the Addictions, 25(4A),* 435-463.

Luepker, R., Johnson, C.A., Murray, D.M., and Pechacek, T.F. (1983). Prevention of cigarette smoking: Three-year follow-up of an education program for youth. *Journal of Behavioral Medicine, 6(1),* 53-62.

Mathias, R. (November/December 1994). School based drug prevention programs show long lasting results. *NIDA Notes.* U.S. Public Health Service (NIH Pub. No. 95-3478), 8-9.

MacKinnon, D.P., Johnson, C.A., Pentz, M.A., Dwyer, J.H., Hansen, W.B., Flay, B.R., and Wang, E.Y. (1991). Mediating mechanisms in a school-based drug prevention program: First-year effects of the Midwestern prevention project. *Health Psychology, 10(3),* 164-172.

McGuire, W.J. (1968). The nature of attitudes and attitude change. In G. Lindzey and E. Aranson (Eds.) *Handbook of Social Psychology.* Reading, Mass: Addison-Wesley.

Moskowitz, J., Malvin, J., Schaeffer, G., and Schaps, E. (1983). Evaluation of a junior high school primary prevention program. *Addictive Behaviors, 8,* 393-401.

Moskowitz, J., Malvin, J., Schaeffer, G., and Schaps. E. (1984a). An experimental evaluation of a drug evaluation course. *Journal of Drug Education, 14(1),* 9-22.

Moskowitz, J., Schaps, E., Malvin, J., and Schaeffer, G. (1984b). The effects of drug education at follow-up. *Journal of Alcohol and Drug Education, 30,* 45-49.

Murray, D., Pirie, P., Luepker, R., and Pallonen, V. (1989). Five and six-year follow-up results from four seventh-grade smoking prevention strategies. *Journal of Behavioral Medicine, 12(2),* 207-218.

Pentz, M.A., Dwyer, J., MacKinnon, D., Flay, B.R., et al. (1989). A multicommunity trial for primary prevention of adolescent drug abuse effects on drug use prevalence. *Journal of the American Medical Association, 261(2),* 3259-3266.

Perry, C. (1987). Results of prevention programs with adolescents. *Drug and Alcohol Dependence, 20,* 13-19.

Perry, C., Grant, M., Ernberg, G., Florenzano, R., et al. (1989). WHO collaborative study on alcohol education and young people: Outcomes of a four-country pilot study. *International Journal of the Addictions, 24(12),* 1145-1171.

Perry, C.J., Killen, L.A., Slinkard, A.L., and McAlister, A. (1980). Peer teaching and smoking prevention among junior high students. *Adolescence, 9,* 277-281.

Rhodes, J.E. and Jason, L.A. (1987). The retrospective pretest: An alternative approach in evaluating drug prevention programs. *Journal of Drug Education, 17,* 345-356.

Schaps, E., DiBartolo, R., Moskowitz, J., Palley, C.S., et al. (1981). A review of 127 drug abuse prevention program evaluations. *Journal of Drug Issues, 11,* 17-43.

Schaps, E., Moskowitz, J., Malvin, J.H., and Schaeffer, G. (1986). Evaluation of seven school-based prevention programs: A final report on the Napa Project. *International Journal of the Addictions, 21,* 1081-1112.

Schinke, S.P., Orlandi, M.A., Botvin, G., Gilchrest, L.D., et al. (1988). Preventing substance abuse among American-Indian adolescents: A bicultural competence skills approach. *Journal of Counseling Psychology, 35(1),* 87-90.

Shedler, J., and Block, J. (1990). Adolescent drug use and psychological health. *American Psychologist, 45(5),* 612-630.

Shope, J.T., Copeland, L.A., Maharg, R., Dielman, T.E., and Butchart, A.T. (1993). Assessment of adolescent refusal skills in an alcohol misuse prevention study. *Health Education Quarterly, 20(3),* 373-390.

Silverman, M.M. (1988). Prevention research: Impediments, barriers, and inadequacies. In *OSAP Prevention Monograph 3 - Prevention Research Findings,* 24-32.

Stein, J.A., Swisher, J.D., Hu, T., and McDonald, N.S. (1984). Cost-effectiveness evaluation of a Channel One program. *Journal of Drug Education, 14(3),* 251-269.

Swan, N. (March/April 1995). Marijuana and other drug use among teens continues to rise. *NIDA Notes.* U. S. Public Health Service (NIH Pub. No. 95-3478), 8-9.

Swisher, J.D., and Hu, T. (1983). Alternatives to drug abuse: Some are and some are not. *N.I.D.A.-Research Monograph Series, 47,* 141-153.

Tobler, N. S. (1986). Meta-analysis of 143 adolescent drug prevention programs: Quantitative outcome results of program participants compared to a control or comparison group. *Journal of Drug Issues, 16(4),* 537-567.

U.S. Public Health Service (Jan. 1995). *National Household Survey on Drug Abuse: Main Findings 1992.* Dept. of Health and Human Services Administration, Office of Applied Studies. DHHS Pub. No.(SMA) 94-3012.

Weisheit, R.A. (1983). The social context of alcohol and drug education: Implications for program evaluations. *Journal of Alcohol and Drug Education, 29,* 72-81.

Wills, T.A., and Shiffman, S. (1985). Coping and substance use: A conceptual framework. In S. Shiffman and T.A. Wills (Eds.) *Coping and Substance Use.* New York: Academic Press.

Wodarski, J. S. (1987). Teaching adolescents about alcohol and driving: A two year follow-up. *Journal of Drug Education, 17(4),* 327-344.

CHAPTER 3

School Climate and Community Norm Change

Sharyn J. Zunz

INTRODUCTION

It's an afterthought. In many books and articles on adolescent substance abuse prevention, the need to change school climate and community norms is discussed only after all the risk factors, personality theories, and diagnoses of dysfunctions have been explored. Only at that point does the reader come across a brief section that describes the importance of efforts to positively influence school climate or change community norms.

This is surprising given two pieces of evidence: First, our curricula-based and school-delivered prevention efforts have yielded only limited long-term success (Dryfoos, 1993a; Ellickson et al., 1993; Ennett et al., 1994). Despite over a decade of school-based programming, substance abuse continues to cost our country $200 billion annually in law enforcement, health care, treatment, and lost productivity (Center for Substance Abuse Prevention, 1993). Second, evidence suggests that the behaviors we have had the most success in reducing over the past decade—smoking, drunk driving, and crack cocaine use—have declined in large part due to the media attention surrounding the negative norms response to these behaviors (Ayres, 1994; Valentich, 1994). For example, there has been a 12 percent decrease in the number of traffic fatalities due to drunk driving—from 57 percent in 1982 to 45 percent in 1992, although there is little evidence that the amount of actual drinking has declined (Ayres, 1994). This can partially be explained because alcohol continues to be our country's drug of choice, while stigma now occurs where alcohol and driving are combined.

The public health field has often been ahead of the social sciences and education in realizing the importance of norm and climate issues.

Practitioners see prevention as a norm changing process "...that empowers individuals and systems to meet the challenges of life events and transitions by creating and reinforcing healthy behavior and lifestyle choices" (Benard, Fafoglia, and McDonald, 1991, p. 92). The surgeon general and the public health community, for example, were the ones to sound the alarm about the dangers of smoking. Their norm change efforts have led to a 10 percent to 15 percent reduction in cigarette consumption since the mid-1960's (Hendrick, 1994). Norm change in regard to cigarette smoking has also produced consequences that were almost unthinkable just fifteen years ago. For example, restrictions now exist on smoking in offices, restaurants, airplanes, and even jail cells (Johnson et al., 1990, Skolnick, 1990, Valentich, 1994).

The consequences of shifting community norms around smoking have also begun to be observed in the political arena. In 1994, Congress felt empowered to hold unprecedented hearings to investigate the practices and potential culpability of the $44 billion American tobacco industry (Hendrick, 1994). In addition, substantial excise taxes on cigarettes and alcohol ("sin taxes") to fund needed government programs have been contemplated by federal and local governments (Christensen, 1994).

There are numerous causes for adolescent substance abuse, and therefore we need to avoid simplistic solutions. No one program component, brief curriculum exposure, or "silver bullet" can be expected to greatly affect the complex and socially derived behaviors of teens. Therefore, effective prevention efforts must target multiple systems and employ multiple strategies. This chapter will explore the importance to prevention programming of one of the most overlooked or undervalued strategies: the strategy that attempts to influence norms, values, and policies. It will expand our prevention focus from the traditional interventions at the "micro" (individual) or "mezzo" (group or family) levels, to strategies at the "macro" levels (schools and communities).

This expansion of focus is important for two reasons. First, adolescence is a developmental period when influences outside the family begin to take on greater significance. Since the number of working parents has increased, children often leave their family's care before breakfast and are not back home before 6 or 7 p.m. even in the elementary school years. This means our country's youth spends most of their waking hours under the influence of entities in the "macro sphere," such as before and after school programs, recreational or community activities, and child-care settings.

Second, a concentration on macro factors moves the prevention field away from examining teens and their families with a "blame the victim" mentality to an environmental focus where every community member has a responsibility to contribute to adolescent substance abuse prevention and general health promotion. A macro focus moves us away from condemning "those trouble-makers."   This is important when we consider that it is probable that almost half of our teen population is at risk for substance abuse problems, delinquency, unsafe sexual practices, and poor school attendance or performance (Dryfoos, 1990, 1993b). This wider view does not look at these at-risk teens as failures but instead examines how we as the community have failed and what we are obligated to do for this group of our community's young people.

This chapter will explore the efforts that have been made at macro-level prevention interventions. It will begin by looking at school programs that are not solely aimed at transmitting substance abuse prevention information but at changing the climate and policies that affect the norms imparted to students. The second part of the chapter will look at norm change from a community standpoint. Since many teens do not attend school or are "turned off" to any messages coming from the school or school personnel, it is important to look to the greater community to provide constructive pathways and resources that can support abuse prevention efforts.

SCHOOL CLIMATE CHANGE

As previously indicated, the major concentration of our country's adolescent substance abuse efforts has been on school-based curricula that deliver some combination of information, self-esteem building, and resistance skills training. But what about the school environment in which these messages are delivered? What messages do children get when the star athlete or mayor's daughter gets differential treatment for substance abuse infractions compared to the rest of a school's students? Or when students who are expelled for drug use are never referred for help? What about alumni events or faculty retirement parties where drinking is the central activity? Or families who are not actively discouraged from serving underage children drinks before the junior prom? Or schools where diversity is not celebrated, where safety is a paramount concern, and where parents do not feel welcome?   All these issues are relevant to substance abuse rates within a school system, yet they are rarely addressed through packaged prevention programs. The thread that encompasses all these issues of concern is the concept of school climate.

School climate may have been avoided as a relevant notion in substance abuse prevention because it is hard to define. It is a qualitative, "soft" concept that describes how people feel in, and about, their school. It is based on impressions, opinions, and beliefs. Keefe defines climate as "... the relatively enduring patterns of shared perceptions about the characteristics of an organization and its members" (Keefe, 1989, p. 36).

Climate can also be defined as characteristics that describe an organization, influence the behavior of people within it, endure over time, and distinguish that organization from the rest of the environment (Johnson et al., 1987). Climate includes a school's physical plant, organizational structure, culture, values, norms, communication patterns, leadership style, and decision-making processes. A school with a positive climate encourages commitment and bonding in its participants.

Social bonding is a protective factor often cited in the drug prevention literature, yet our schools' climates often make this type of bonding difficult (Hawkins et al., 1992; Kumpfer and Turner, 1990). Meier (1993) tells of a group of recent high school dropouts who were interviewed about whether they ever met anyone who was a college graduate. The students almost unanimously said "no" even though all of them had previously attended schools with teachers and other school personnel who were all college graduates. It was clear that these former students had no real or lasting connection with any of the school's employees since when questioned, they either failed to come to mind or the ex-students were unaware of the educational qualifications required for these jobs. These former students had inhabited the same physical space but not the same world as the adults around them. This lack of connection was confirmed in a study by Naginey and Swisher (1990) in which 7th to 12th-grade students said if they had a drug-related concern, they would go to peers (84.6 percent) or adult friends (73 percent) significantly more often than they would turn to school counselors (34.6 percent), teachers (21.5 percent), or school administrators (9.6 percent).

The climate in many of our junior and senior high schools is very impersonal. Secondary schools are one of the few institutions in our society in which people are forced to change their activity, peer group, and instructors every 45-50 minutes (Meier, 1993). Moreover, until recently, school orientation programs have been inadequate, which has made the transition to both middle and high schools a time of increased risk for substance abuse (Linney and Brondino, 1993; Price et al., 1993).

Comer's Model

James Comer, a child psychiatrist with the Yale Child Study Center, was one of the first to identify the importance of school climate through his work with the New Haven, Connecticut, school system (Comer, 1993; Payne, 1991). Comer began in the 1960s in two inner-city public elementary schools that had low achievement scores; poor attendance; children with increasing anti-social behavior patterns; and low morale on the part of parents, staff, and students. Poor parents and parents of color were particularly alienated from schools that they found to be insensitive, ineffective, and blaming. Due to his success in turning these schools around, Comer's model had been duplicated in ten school districts nationwide by 1990 (Anson et al., 1991; Payne, 1991).

There is fairly extensive coverage of Comer's philosophy, programs, and outcomes in the education literature (Anson et al., 1991; Comer, 1993; Comer and Haynes, 1991; Payne, 1991). His philosophy was to examine the individual school as well as the school system as a whole and to improve their climates. His efforts avoided any concentration on changing an individual or group of students, teachers, or families.

The two cornerstones of his attempts to improve school climate were school-based management structures and enhanced family involvement. To achieve these ends, his programs developed three components: School Planning and Management Teams, Mental Health Teams, and Family Programs. A brief description of the implementation of these components is as follows:

1. School Planning and Management Teams—These teams were composed of school administrators, teachers, support staff, and family members. (Students were also given representation at the junior and senior high levels.) Each team's mission was to develop a comprehensive school plan to improve both academics and school climate without paralyzing or undercutting the principal's ability to function. The teams were to model collaborative efforts, constructive problem solving, and consensus building. Every meeting was to be

task oriented, with a specific agenda that provided a sense of direction and enhanced a sense of ownership of school programs and buildings.

2. Mental Health Teams—These teams consisted of school\guidance counselors, psychologists, social workers, and special education teachers. Their functions were not just to help individual students and their families when special needs arose but to be proactive and preventive by recommending changes to the School Planning and Management Team to improve the general health\mental health of the school community. Their interventions were to focus on developmental issues and relationship problems common to most students in their facilities. They were not to label individual students as "high risk."

The Mental Health Team was to look at issues like mutual respect, safety on school property, and sensitivity to diversity issues. In addition, Mental Health Teams worked with the Family Programs to develop community service projects for the middle and high school students.

3. Family Programs—Connecting, reconnecting, and maintaining connections by families to the local school were viewed as crucial. Comer wanted parents to feel useful, knowledgeable, and valued. He began by reaching out to parents for help with school social events, class trips, and planning the school calendar. Families were also included in developing adult education classes that the school might offer as desired by the community.

In addition, several assemblies were scheduled to encourage parents to come to school and see their children perform and be publicly recognized. Parents were also encouraged to contribute to the school's cultural life by bringing their personal stories and ethnic observances to school events. These school functions were part of an overall effort to give parents a positive experience within the school—a place to reverse the perception of the school as a forbidding place to only hear "bad news." These endeavors included scheduling special fathers' breakfast events as well as other activities accessible to working parents. Principals in some districts called local employers to ask for their cooperation in allowing family members release time to attend school functions or to ask for corporate space during employees' lunch hours to hold school planning meetings. The goal was to somehow involve 100 percent of the students' families at some level during the school year (Anson et al., 1991; Comer and Haynes, 1991).

The next step was to enlist about 5 percent to 10 percent of the parents as parental aids or paraprofessional assistants to the school. It was important that these assignments be meaningful to the school's functioning and not just tokenism. Parents were involved not only in academic functions but in the development of life skills curricula, including teaching neighborhood survival competencies, understanding local politics, health promotion strategies, budgeting, personal finance, and business ownership; and promoting connections to local spiritual and recreational resources (Comer and Haynes, 1991).

The last step was to recruit five or six parents who might be interested in being on the School Planning and Management Team or running for the local school board. It was important for these parents to feel a sense of ownership toward their local school and to understand that they were sharing in an accountability process. In addition, these parents served as community links for school personnel who often did not reside in the school districts or come from the same socio-economic or ethnic background as their students.

Comer's attempts to influence school climate were not without difficulties. School personnel were initially unsupportive of many of his ideas because they did not want to share power and they did not trust the parents' competence to fulfill their responsibilities (especially on school governance teams). There were problems with union rules and contracts, with failure to train parents on confidentiality issues, with lack of role clarity, and with personality style mismatches between parent aids and school personnel (Comer and Haynes, 1991).

However, despite the above-named problems, attempts to influence school climate using Comer's and other similar models have been successful (Anson et al., 1991; Haynes et al., 1989). Children in the schools where the climate is positive observe the conduct of the parents and teachers and then begin to bond to the pro-social values they see demonstrated. Students who have their strengths and abilities confirmed and recognized in an ethnically and gender sensitive manner displayed more positive mental health behaviors. Researchers found that positive school climates in which children and their families felt heard and respected reduced the attraction of substance abuse and other anti-social behaviors (Kumpfer and Turner, 1990). In addition, researchers found that in schools in which the rules and policies around smoking were clear, fairly enforced, and concentrated on prevention over punishment, the prevalence rate as well as the average amount of smoking were lowered (Pentz, Brannon et al., 1989).

Measurement of School Climate

Since Comer's original work, there have been attempts by researchers to develop measures for this "fuzzy" notion of school climate. For example, the Charles F. Kettering School Climate profile (CFK) was developed with eight subscales to measure a school's ability to foster respect, trust, morale, opportunity for input, academic and social growth, cohesiveness, renewal, and caring (Johnson et al., 1987).

Gottfredson and Hollifield (1988) developed another measure, an inventory, the Effective School Battery (ESB), to measure school climate. The ESB included surveys of elements like safety, morale, a school's ability to plan and take action on important issues, sound school administration, sufficient resources, positive race relations, parental and community commitment to the school, and a place for students to feel empowered. Using the ESB, Gottfredson and Hollifield (1988) found schools with good psychosocial and academic climates had teachers who reported the following: feeling safe on school grounds, job satisfaction, orderly but interactive classrooms with good student\teacher rapport, staff opportunities for professional growth and development, and nonauthoritarian school administration. Students in schools with positive school climate scores had positive peer associations, parents who supported their academic efforts, attachment and pride in their school, investment in the equitably enforced school rules and regulations, and an expectation that they would have at least some success in school.

A third attempt to construct a measurement of school climate and its consequences was developed through the National Association of Secondary School Principals (NASSP). This instrument, the Comprehensive Assessment of School Environment (CASE), consists of 10 scales (Keefe, 1989):

1. Teacher-student relationships
2. Student-peer relationships
3. Students' values
4. Students' academic orientation
5. Student activities
6. Guidance\counseling functions
7. Teaching quality

8. Administration and leadership
9. Security and maintenance
10. Parent, community, and school relationships.

This instrument uses statements to elicit answers from respondents on various questions (Coladarci and Donaldson, 1991). What happens when a child does something good or bad in school? Does the principal really care? Does the school make students want to learn? Does the school foster respect between and among students, families, and school personnel? The goal of CASE is to measure a school's physical and social environmental conditions, the students' awareness and conformity to pro-social norms, the level of parental and community involvement, and the supportiveness of the school environment for personnel.

All three of these measurements have been used in the educational field over the past decade, but this author was unable to find any studies where these scales were used in conjunction with substance abuse prevention efforts. One could anticipate (all other factors remaining constant), that as schools improved their scores on school climate scales, their drug abuse prevention efforts would be more successful and their level of substance abuse related problems would diminish. Future attempts at interdisciplinary research might yield some fruitful findings in this area.

Student Assistance Programs (SAP's)
School climate can be improved through increased student participation and ownership of a school's health\mental health programming. One of the ways this has been accomplished is through Student Assistance Programs. SAP's were begun in schools more than 20 years ago as a means to deal with student problems that included their own, their peer's, and their family's substance abuse (McGovern and Dupont, 1991). Student Assistance Programs (SAP's) were based on the models of Employee Assistance Programs (EAP's) that handle personal problems in the work place that hinder productivity.

SAP's are collaborative efforts between groups of students, teachers, parents, school personnel, and community resources. They are sometimes part of a larger comprehensive school-based multi-service center set up to address student health\mental health problems (Dryfoos, 1993b). SAP's represent a range of approaches to substance abuse prevention but generally include some combination of the following (McGovern and DuPont, 1991; Moore and Foster, 1993):

1) Identifying\training students to be peer counselors.
2) Identifying students who are having, or are at
   risk of having, substance abuse problems.
3) Referring students to professional services.
4) Coordinating school re-entry efforts for students
   returning from residential drug\alcohol treatment.
5) Running student rap groups, parent support groups,
   and coordinating with programs like Alateen and
   Students Against Drunk Driving (SADD).
6) Acting as consultants to school personnel on
   substance abuse policy issues and on ways
   schools can build protective influences against
   risk behaviors.

As with other programs to improve school climate, SAP's have not been without their problems. Issues of school liability, student confidentiality, cost, and use of the program as a law\rule enforcement vehicle are some common problems. However, research is beginning to show the ability of SAP's to decrease the academic and social problems of its participants as well as improve school climate (Cooley, 1993; Moore and Foster, 1993).

Other Examples of School Climate Change

A multiyear adolescent substance abuse prevention project funded by the State of New York in the early 1990s reviewed many ongoing attempts by a variety of practitioners to positively influence school climate (Norman et al., 1994). Although programs based on Comer's school climate change model and student assisted\peer counselors programs were two of the most common, other interventions were as follows.

1. Several school districts used their sports teams, cheerleaders, and pep squads to deliver drug free and health–promotion messages to students.

2. Efforts to control substance abuse during graduation and proms were common. Substance free after-prom events were planned with the cooperation of the school and town. In one district, the parents, school, and prevention community got together to warn limousine drivers and car services of their potential liability in allowing

underage youth to become intoxicated in their vehicles when riding to and from proms.

3. After a local student was killed in a drunk driving accident, the school organized a DWI awareness day. Local auto body and salvage shops donated cars destroyed in drunk driving accidents to be displayed in front of the school. During the day the school bell rang at exactly the rate that someone is killed in the United States due to a substance abuse related accident. Each time the school bell rang a student donned a black memorial arm band. In addition, an assembly was held where a community safe rides program was discussed.

The important point of all of the work on school climate is to indicate what can be done to make the school as an entity part of a community's substance abuse prevention strategy. Whether one's efforts are through a Student Assistance or Peer Counselor program, an athletic program, drug-free proms, or a more holistic attempt to change the total school environment like the Comer Model, the crucial thing is to make substance abuse prevention more than a series of lectures in health class or an assembly. School climate change is the way to show teens we mean to "walk the walk, not just talk the talk."

COMMUNITY NORM CHANGE

One's community by definition should be a place where one belongs, feels nurtured, and is encouraged to develop healthful habits (Benard, 1993; Blyth and Roehlkepartain, 1993; Keith, 1993). Therefore, community is not just defined by geographic or geopolitical boundaries but by a state of positive identification and connectedness. Communities also transmit norms to their members. Norms are defined as common beliefs and expectations about appropriate behavior that guide our interactions with others (Schriver, 1995). Norms, whether they be formal\informal or explicit\implicit, give our communities a sense of stability and unity over time (Longres, 1995).

A healthy community should be a place where caring, commitment, and mutual protection are the norm. It is clear that when we fail to provide our youth with such a setting, they will invent a community of their own with potentially anti-social values and norms. For example, street gangs through their secret codes, club colors, jackets, and pledges of mutual dependency supply their members with a sense of community they find lacking elsewhere. Gangs supply youth with structure, a place to contribute, and tangible rewards.

Although we talk about adolescent substance abuse as a societal and/or community problem, we rarely look at how our larger social institutions affect this issue. Past community efforts have run into difficulty because they have been one or more of the following (Linquanti, 1992; Pittman, 1991):

1) Reactive and crisis oriented
2) Rigid and bureaucratic
3) Fragmented, competitive, and uncooperative
4) Label, turf, and problem driven and
5) Plagued by duplication in some arenas with
   gaps in others.

This section will explore some past and present efforts to address substance abuse prevention on a community level. It will look at what we have learned from these attempts and how community strategies might be better employed.

Since the latest "war on drugs" began, our society has made many attempts to tackle substance abuse on the "macro" level through efforts at supply and demand reduction (Center for Substance Abuse Prevention, 1993). On the supply reduction front, our major efforts have been in law enforcement. For example, we have attempted to lower drunk driving rates by raising the drinking age, through more sophisticated and frequent Driving While Intoxicated (DWI) police checkpoints, by stricter punishments for impaired drivers (administrative license revocation for failing a sobriety test is now common in over 35 states), and by holding bar owners, bartenders, and party hosts responsible for their guests (Ayres, 1994; Hawkins et al., 1992). We have tried to reduce the drug supply through tougher sentencing laws and international interdiction efforts. However, according to the government's Center for Substance Abuse Prevention (1993), although we almost doubled our law enforcement efforts in the 1980s, we were unsuccessful in creating any significant drug scarcity on the street level (the price of cocaine actually went down by 25 percent during this time period).

As we were concentrating on efforts to reduce supply, we began to pull back from any serious focus on reducing demand. It has become more and more clear to policy makers in an era of federal budget deficits that reducing demand through treatment of abusers is a costly and time consuming process. Even with the rarity of available and good quality treatment, the recidivism rate can be as high as 2 of 3 in first attempts at rehabilitation (CSAP, 1993). Therefore, societal attempts to tackle substance abuse should return to a focus on preventive strategies at the community level that can change norms and save both lives and dollars (Ellickson et al., 1993; Mills, 1992; Pentz et al., 1989).

Social Bonding

There is almost universal agreement in the adolescent substance abuse prevention literature on the merit of providing teens an opportunity for bonding to prosocial individuals and societal norms (Norman et al., 1994). Social bonding is an attachment to community norms which helps an individual accept socially approved values and clarifies the expectation and consequences of behavior (Bogenschneider et al., 1991). It occurs through an attachment to peers, significant adults, school, religious institutions, and\or communities that convey limits while promoting an investment in oneself and the future of one's community. Assuming that facilitating social bonding is desirable, how can communities and school systems encourage this process?

The goal is to find a way for schools and communities to use social bonding to encourage healthy behaviors. In order for this to successfully take place, several components must be present (Center for Substance Abuse Prevention, 1993; Hawkins et al., 1992):

1. Clarity about the norms and standards to which we expect youth to bond—Norm clarification is often a difficult process for a community to undertake. However, since only a clear and consistent message will yield predictable behavior, it is important for communities to decide which of two messages they wish to convey: a message of total abstinence or one of moderate, appropriate, and legal use. This decision must be made in the context of community, religious, and cultural norms as well as family\personal values and beliefs. Whatever the decision, certain messages to youth should be clear:

a) There are circumstances where no use is the only choice, i.e., illicit drugs or drinking if you are underage, pregnant, or driving.

b) Everyone has the right to make a personal choice not to use substances, and it is always wrong to pressure anyone else to use. Youths should be helped to develop a plan for what they will do when confronted with pressure to use.

c) Substances should never be used to the point of intoxication or when use negatively impacts others.

d) Substance use should never be the center of a social activity or considered essential to having a good time.

2. Youth must have an opportunity to contribute—As was discussed in the school climate section above, no one will bond to the norms of a community to which they do not feel that they belong or where they are not part of the decision-making process. Therefore, opportunities to participate are crucial. These opportunities must be carefully planned. If they are too easy or not meaningful, youth will get bored. If they are too difficult and not age appropriate, youth will give up or fail. Opportunities should allow youths not only to participate with pro-social adults and peers, but also allow them to influence and have access to leadership positions as well as feel capable, empowered, valued, and socially useful.

3. Youths must have the chance to learn and develop skills—Opportunities in and of themselves will not be useful if the teenagers do not have the ability to take advantage of them. Whether it is an academic skill like reading and math or social, communications, or problem-solving skills, children must be prepared if they are to take advantage of prosocial opportunities that present themselves.

4. Recognition—no one wants to do something for nothing. If we want our youth to develop pro-social behaviors and give up or forego unhealthy habits, we must make the rewards and incentives both meaningful and visible. Communities must be able to answer the question teens commonly ask: "What's in it for me and\or mine?"

5. Significant and valued adults in the community must demonstrate concern and commitment if we want youth to become attached. This means adults must communicate (Center for Substance Abuse Prevention, 1993):

a) Concern, care, and the fact that youth are important.

b) A watchful and observant demeanor. In one study, one-half of the teens said it was unlikely that anyone would notice or report their binge drinking behavior, while over 70 percent said they would not continue to binge drink if a significant adult was likely to "find them out" (Bogenschneider, 1991). At least on some level, many teens want to be helped to stop making unhealthy choices.

c) Attention both to words and actions.

d) The ability to separate what is felt about behavior from what is felt about the person.

e) What they realistically can do to support youth in their efforts.

In summary, social bonding requires the 3 "A's": 1) *Aid* through the provision of concrete, practical, and material support; 2) *Affirmation* through feedback that raises self-esteem and promotes positive identity formation; and 3) *Affect* that communicates nuturance and caring (Price et al., 1993).

Examples of Community-Based Programs

Over the past decade, there have been several attempts on the part of community-based substance abuse prevention programs to address the issues of norm change and social bonding. Below are some examples:

1. *Youth Charters* (Benard, 1993). In several communities, adult and teen leaders have forged alliances to develop "youth charters" that spell out the expectations that both teens and the adults will promote healthful behaviors. To be successful these charters must make meaningful participation possible for the diverse elements of the community and must be prepared to formally evaluate their progress towards agreed upon goals.

2. *Midwestern Prevention Program* (Johnson et al., 1990; Pentz et al., 1989). In Kansas City and other locations, full-scale and integrated community-based programs to reduce substance use were initiated. These programs including regulations, enforcement, and norm-change efforts in schools, workplaces, and community events. They also enlisted the help of the local media and sports figures and celebrities. These programs were able to demonstrate reductions in tobacco and marijuana use.

3. *Modello/Homestead Project* (Benard and Lorio, 1991; Mills, 1992). This project was undertaken in a low income and crime-ridden Florida housing complex. The intervention used a holistic

approach to provide community leadership training, change school climate, coordinate multiple agency efforts, and encourage job development and community empowerment. The project reported success in lowering drug traffic in the housing project by 65 percent and lowering substance abuse rates by 50 percent.

Similar housing-project-based programs have been undertaken by the Boys and Girls Clubs. These endeavors, called "Smart Moves," stress adult involvement and have been successful in lowering drug activity and drug abuse, curbing property damage, and lowering gang activity (Pittman, 1991).

4. *Project RAISE* (Benard, 1992; Nettles, 1992). This project uses coaches or mentors to encourage teens to engage in healthful behavior. The coaches' tasks are to facilitate the learning of a competency that improves self-esteem, to promote a positive cultural and ethnic identity, and to advocate for their mentees in their school and community environments.

There have been many other similar school- or community-based mentoring programs: Eugene Lange's "I Have a Dream" (provides college scholarships and mentors to prevent high school drop outs), Las Madrinas (provides working Latina "godmothers" to teenage girls), and Project Spirit sponsored by the Congress of National Black Churches (Price et al., 1993).

5. *Search Institute-Healthy Communities* (Blyth and Roehlkepartain, 1993). This was a research project which studied 112 different community groups serving 9th to 12th graders. The findings were as follows:

a) In all the communities they surveyed from the least to the most healthful, only 1/3 of the youths questioned said they had a non-parental adult to whom they felt positively connected.

b) A healthy community environment protects not only high-functioning youth but vulnerable youth as well. Vulnerable youth in functional communities exhibit only 41 percent of the high-risk behaviors observed in similar youth in less healthy communities without pro-social norm and social bonding opportunities.

c) There is a threshold effect. Where there are many risk factors for unhealthful behaviors in a community, there must be a critical mass of coordinated and integrated community interventions before teens receive a positive benefit.

6. *Harvard Alcohol Project* (Dejong and Winsten, 1990). This project focused on the use of the media to change community norms around drunk driving and to promote designated-driver programs. It took place during the holiday seasons in 1988 through 1990 and used public service announcements (PSA'S) plus an appeal to top-rated TV programs to use drinking and driving in their plot lines. A follow-up indicated that 78 percent of drivers saw at least one of these PSA's or TV shows. They also found that their efforts along with others undertaken at this time resulted in a 10 percent to 15 percent increase in designated-driver use.

Through this project and similar research efforts, these authors offer the following suggestions in using media to reduce teen substance abuse:

a) Media should target gateway substances for pre-teens (tobacco, alcohol, and marijuana) and promote postponement of experimentation.

b) Media should show benefits of a healthy lifestyle and attack misperceptions about the prevalence and effects of substance use. Advertise the appeal of non-using peers and activities. Media should not only advocate the need for healthful change but also support those already struggling to maintain a healthy lifestyle.

c) Media should avoid fear tactics and build on short-term motivations relevant to teens, i.e., attractiveness to potential partners or desire for personal freedom and autonomy in decision-making.

d) Media should promote not only knowledge acquisition but ways to change behaviors. This should include resistance skills and self-management techniques to sustain behavior changes. This can include the use of celebrities or corporate sponsors whose products are popular with teens.

Lessons on Organizing Community-Based Projects

For the writing of this chapter, a review of the community organization literature that reflected attempts to change social norms and promote social bonding in teens was undertaken (Benard, 1986; Cazares and Beatty, 1994; Center for Substance Abuse Prevention, 1993; Keith, 1993; Leukefeld and Bukoski, 1991; Office of Substance Abuse Prevention, 1991; Price et al., 1993; Wiebel, 1993). There are several consistent threads in this literature as well as in the findings on the programs just described. Since these themes may provide useful lessons for those contemplating a community-based adolescent substance abuse prevention program, a synthesis of the suggestions from this literature is provided below:

1. Multiple and comprehensive strategies work best. Adolescent substance abuse should not be isolated from other community problems. In addition, efforts must reach out to gain cooperation and collaboration from all segments of the community, including teens, families, significant adults, workplaces, and all community groups and leaders.

2. Community-based interventions must examine the potential consequences of their efforts. For example, a crackdown on drug use by teen athletes could lead to suspensions of players, lost revenues, more lost games, and possible loss of sports scholarships. Is the community going to be willing to continue to back up the program if these consequences occur?

3. Begin with a focused, specific, and localized needs assessment which reaches all key informants. If it's not local and specific, many will continue to deny problems exist by saying "not here." Also, research on needs assessments generally find that most communities overestimate their illicit drug problems and underestimate their alcohol-related problems.

4. Don't reinvent the wheel. Most communities have had some form of adolescent substance abuse prevention initiatives in the past. Find out what has been tried, who were "the players," what were the outcomes, and what resources are already in place. A lack of duplication is especially important in a period of limited resources.

5. Set small, realistic, well-defined, and measurable goals. For example, it is unrealistic to say you are going to eliminate teenage drinking. Instead, sample goals could be to lower the drunk driving rate among teens, delay onset of alcohol use, or reduce alcohol-related sexual assault incidents.

6. Programs should be targeted to the developmental level of the teens involved. It is also crucial for programs to be both sensitive and competent on issues of gender, race, class, and ethnicity. This includes an understanding of language, acculturation, gender roles, and cultural myths, symbols, and rites of passage.

7. Community efforts have known pitfalls that should be anticipated and require proactive planning. Some of the most common ones cited in the research were chronically inadequate funding and availability of needed resources, turf battles with both

inter- and intra-group fighting, and resistance in engaging some teens and their families.

8. Poverty and discrimination are at the root of many community problems. Efforts to address the effects of these realities on adolescents should not be ignored. For example, this author knows of an inner-city youth who was treasurer of his drug-free, community-sponsored club. After he was questioned suspiciously at a local bank because he came in with a large cash deposit from the club's fundraiser, he stopped attending the club meetings and began to associate with more anti-social peers.

9. The use of indigenous staff for adolescent substance abuse prevention programs is often desirable. However, these staff members must be chosen carefully. They should be able to relate to the target community, serve as constructive role models, be effective communicators, and be seen as positive representatives of the program and its goals.

10. Include a research component. Good research on community-based risk and protective factors as well as community interventions is one of the greatest deficiencies in the adolescent substance abuse prevention field. There is very little research that sees the community, not the individual, as the unit of service.

CONCLUSION

As we head towards the next century, certain lessons from our long struggle against substance abuse should be clear: an approach that focuses only on supply reduction is doomed to failure, prevention is the only humane and cost-effective route, and prevention efforts must be multidimensional. In addition, in an era of concern over deficit spending at all government levels, it is unlikely that sufficient funds for adequate and accessible treatment will be forthcoming for all who are in need. Furthermore, the current political climate is one of returning whatever funding is available to programs managed at the local, not federal, level. All of these realities point to the increased need on the part of preventionists to look towards school climate and community norm change as a crucial part of the substance abuse prevention arsenal. These interventions can no longer be an afterthought to curriculum-based or individual risk reduction efforts.

Given the political realities described above and after reviewing the literature for this chapter, this author has several other observations about future "macro"-level substance abuse prevention efforts. First, there is no need to reinvent the wheel. Efforts (some of which are outlined in this chapter) already underway can serve as guides to school- and community-based programs. Second, as much as we may long for the days of schools whose sole focus was on the 3 R's and families with stay-at-home moms, those days are gone forever. As children spend more time away from their working parents, it is increasingly clear that it will "take a whole village to raise a child." This means that school- and community-based programs must be used to reduce risk behaviors in our children.

In addition, we need to increase our ability to do prevention research on the "macro" level. Until we are able to better document the success of broad-based interventions, we cannot hope to compete for the limited dollars allocated for these much needed services. And finally, it is urgent that we find a way to make substance abuse prevention a truly multidisciplinary undertaking. Turf battles between professions will only hinder our efforts and set a bad example of factionalism for the schools and communities we are trying to unite.

REFERENCES

Anson, A., Cook, T., Habib, R., Grady, M., Haynes, N., and Comer, J. (1991). The Comer School development program: A theoretical analysis. *Urban Education, 26(1),* 56-82.

Ayres, B.D. (May 22, 1994). Big gains are seen in battle to stem drunken driving. *New York Times,* A1.

Benard, B. (1986). Characteristics of effective prevention programs. *Prevention Forum, 6(4),* 3-8.

Benard, B. (1987). A fall review of four exemplary prevention models. *Prevention Forum, 8(1),* 1.

Benard, B. (1992). Mentoring programs for urban youth: Handle with care. San Francisco, Calif: Far West Lab. for Educational Research and Development, unpublished manuscript.

Benard, B. (December 1993). Weaving the fabric of resiliency in communities. *Western Center News,* San Francisco, Calif: Far West Laboratory for Educational Research and Development, 13.

Benard, B., and Lorio, R. (June 1991). Positive approach to social ills has promise. *Western Center News,* San Francisco, Calif: Far West Laboratory for Educational Research and Development, 1.

Benard, B., Fafogla, B., and McDonald, M. (1991). Effective substance abuse prevention: School social workers as catalysts for change. *Social Work in Education, 13(2),* 90-104.

Blyth, D., and Roehlkepartain, E. (1993). *Healthy Communities, Healthy Youth.* Minneapolis, Minn: Search Institute.

Bogenschneider, K., Small, S., and Riley, D. (1991). *An Ecological, Risk-focused Approach for Addressing Youth-at-risk Issues.* Chevy Chase, Md: National 4-H Center.

Cazares, A. and Beatty, L. (Eds.). (1994). *Scientific Methods for Prevention Intervention Research.* NIDA research monograph # 139. Rockville, Md: NIDA.

Center for Substance Abuse Prevention (1993). *Everybody's Business: Drug-free Schools and Communities.* Rockville, Md.: U.S. Dept. of Health & Human Services, CSAP.

Christensen, M. (March 6, 1994). Tobacco lobby tries to hold back the tide. *The Atlanta Constitution,* A10.

Coladarci, T., and Donaldson, G. (September 1991). Improving school climate: School climate assessment encourages collaboration. *NASSP Bulletin, 91,* 111-119.

Comer, J., and Haynes, N. (1991). Parent involvement in schools: An ecological approach. *Elementary School Journal, 91(3),* 271- 277.

Comer, J. (1993). *A Brief History and Summary of the School Development Program (1992-1993).* New Haven, Conn: Yale Child Study Center.

Cooley, V. (1993). Tips for implementing student assistance programs. *NASSP Bulletin, 76(549),* 10-20.

Dejong, W., and Winsten, J. (1990). The use of mass media in substance abuse prevention. *Health Affairs, 9,* 30-46.

Dryfoos, J. (1990). *Adolescents at Risk: Prevalence and Prevention.* New York: Oxford University Press.

Dryfoos, J. (1993a). Preventing substance use: Rethinking strategies. *American Journal of Public Health, 83 (6),* 793-795.

Dryfoos, J. (1993b). Schools as places for health, mental health, and social services. *Teachers College Record, 94(3),* 540-567.

Ellickson, P., Bell, R., and McGuigan, K. (1993). Preventing Adolescent drug use: Long-term results of a junior high program. *American Journal of Public Health, 83(6),* 856-861.

Ennett, S., Tobler, N., Ringwalt, C., and Flewelling, R. (1994). How effective is drug abuse resistance education: A meta-analysis of project DARE outcome evaluations. *American Journal of Public Health, 84 (9),* 1394-1401.

Gottfredson, G., and Hollifield, J. (1988). How to diagnose school climate: Pinpointing problems, planning change. *NASSP Bulletin, 72(506),* 63-70.

Hawkins, J., Catalano, R., and Miller, J. (1992). Risk and protective factors for alcohol and other drug problems in adolescents and early adulthood: Implications for substance abuse prevention. *Psychological Bulletin, 112(1),* 64-105.

Haynes, N., Comer, J., and Hamilton-Lee, M. (1989). School climate enhancement through parental involvement. *Journal of Social Psychology, 27,* 87-90.

Hendrick, B. (March 6, 1994). Special report: Smoking under siege. *The Atlanta Journal\Atlanta Constitution,* A1.

Johnson, C., Pentz, M., Weber, M., Dwyer, J., and Faly, B. (1990). Relative effectiveness of comprehensive community programming in drug abuse prevention with high-risk and low-risk adolescents. *Journal of Consulting and Clinical Psychology, 58(4),* 447-456.

Johnson, W., Dixon, P., and Robinson, J. (1987). The Charles F. Kettering Ltd. School Climate Instrument: A psychometric analysis. *Journal of Experimental Education, 56(1),* 36-41.

Keefe, J. (1989). Assessing the environment of your school: The NASSP Case model. *NASSP Bulletin, 73(515),* 35-43.

Keith, J. (1993). *Building and Maintaining Community Coalitions on Behalf of Children, Youth and Families.* East Lansing, Mich.: Michigan State University Institute for Children, Youth, and Families, Report #529.

Kumpfer, K., and Turner, C. (1990). The social ecology model of adolescent substance abuse: Implications for prevention. *International Journal of Addictions, 25(4A),* 435-463.

Leukefeld, C., and Bukoski, W. (1991). *Drug Abuse Prevention Intervention Research: Methodological Issues.* NIDA research monograph #107. Rockville, Md: NIDA.

Linney, A., and Brondino, M. (1993). School transition among youth at risk for substance abuse. Paper presented at the 60th biennial meeting of the Society for Research in Child Development, New Orleans, La., March 25-28, 1993.

Linquanti, R. (1992). *Using Community-wide Collaboration to Foster Resiliency in Kids: A Conceptual Framework.* Portland, Ore.: Northwest Regional Educational Lab.

Longres, J. (1995). *Human Behavior in the Social Environment,* 2nd ed. Itasca, Ill.: E.F. Peacock Publishers, Inc.

McDonald, L., Braddish, D., Billingham, S., Dibble, N., and Rice,C. (1991). Families and schools together: An innovative substance abuse prevention program. *Social Work in Education, 13(2),* 118-128.

McGovern, J., and DuPont, R. (1991). Student assistance programs: An important approach to drug abuse prevention. *Journal of School Health, 61(6),* 260-264.

Meier, D. (1993). Transforming schools into powerful communities. *Teachers College Record, 94(3),* 654-660.

Mills, R. (1992). Towards a comprehensive model for prevention: A new foundation for understanding the root causes of drug abuse. Paper presented at the Annual Grantee Meeting, Office for Treatment Improvement-Special Initiatives Branch, New Orleans, La., March 31, 1992.

Moore, D., and Foster, J. (1993). Student assistance programs: New approaches for reducing adolescent substance abuse. *Journal of Counseling & Development, 71,* 326-329.

Naginey, J., and Swisher, J. (December/January 1990). To whom do adolescents turn with drug problems? *The High School Journal,* 80-85.

Nettles, S. M. (1992). *Coaching in Community Settings: A Review.* Boston, Mass: Center on Families, Communities, Schools and Children's Learning.

Norman, E., Turner, S., and Zunz, S.J. (1994). *Substance Abuse Prevention: A Review of the Literature.* New York: Office of Alcohol and Substance Abuse Services.

Office for Substance Abuse Prevention (1991). *The Future by Design: A Community Framework for Preventing Alcohol and Other Drug Problems Through a Systems Approach.* Rockville, Md: OSAP.

Payne, C. (1991). The Comer intervention model and school reform in Chicago: Implications of two models of change. *Urban Education, 26(1),* 8-24.

Pentz, M., Brannon, B., Charlin, V., Barrett, E., Mackinnon, D., and Flay, B. (1989). The power of policy: The relationship of smoking policy to adolescent smoking. *American Journal ofPublic Health, 79(7),* 857-861.

Pentz, M., Dwyer, J., and MacKinnon, D. (1989). A multi community trial for primary prevention of adolescent drug abuse effects on drug use prevalence. *Journal of the American Medical Association, 261(22),* 3259-3266.

Pittman, K. (1991). *Promoting Youth Development: Strengthening the Role of Youth Serving and Community Organizations.* Washington, D.C.: Center for Youth Development and Policy Research.

Price, R., Cioci, M., Penner, W., and Trautlein, B. (1993). Webs of influence: School and community programs that enhance adolescent health and education. *Teachers College Record, 94(3),* 487-521.

Schriver, J. (1995). *Human Behavior and the Social Environment.* Boston: Allyn and Bacon.

Skolnick, A. (1990). Jail leads prisons in smoking ban. *Journal of the American Medical Association, 264,* 1514.

Turner, S., Norman, E., and Zunz, S.J. (1993). *From Risk to Resiliency: A Paradigm Shift.* New York: Fordham University.

Valentich, M. (1994). Social work and the development of a smoke-free society. *Social Work, 39(4),* 439-450.

Wiebel, W. (1993). *The Indigenous Leader Outreach Model: Intervention Manual.* Rockville, Md: NIDA.

CHAPTER 4

New Directions: Looking at Psychological Dimensions in Resiliency Enhancement

Elaine Norman

Most of the school- and community-based substance abuse prevention programs discussed in previous chapters target youngsters who are at relatively low risk for tobacco, alcohol, or other drug use. Most adolescents are abstainers or limited recreational users. There are, however, a sizeable number of youngsters biologically, psychologically and environmentally at high risk for substance abuse. For example, any child of an alcoholic is at higher risk for alcoholism than a child of a non-alcoholic. Youngsters living in economic deprivation and/or in crime and violence prone neighborhoods, and having dysfunctional families have a greater risk of substance abuse than those who do not. A long list of behavioral and psychological factors associated with high risk for substance abuse can also be assembled, including such things as poor school performance and absenteeism and high tolerance for deviant or impulsive behaviors. Dryfoos (1990) estimates that seven million, or 25 percent, of youngsters between the ages of ten and seventeen in the United States today are at high risk for becoming substance abusers.

Prevention programs developed for such individuals are usually based on models of pathology. As such they strive to eliminate or to reduce negative factors that have been shown to be associated with high risk for substance abuse. They focus on working with such things as depression, pessimism, alienation, hyperactivity, social withdrawal, anxiety, impulsivity, and impatience or with aspects of family dysfunction. Such interventions often help to stem the tide of negative stressors in youngster's lives. That task, however, in our modern society is overwhelming and seemingly never ending.

A relatively new and definitely more hopeful focus has appeared on the prevention scene in recent years, *resiliency enhancement*. Very much like seeing a glass which is 50 percent filled with water as half full, rather than half empty, resiliency enhancement programs attempt to enhance factors that protect against vulnerability and "enable sustained competent functioning" even in the presence of major life stressors (Masten et al., 1990). Interventions target enhancing the remarkable capacity of youngsters to withstand considerable hardship, to bounce back in the face of great difficulty and deprivation, and to achieve "competence and strength despite the presence of (considerable) adversities" (Garmezy, 1987).

Many strands of scholarship have met to create this new focus. First, a renewed emphasis on the ecological approach or person-environment interaction reminded us that, in order to understand behavior, persons need to be considered in the context of their environment.

Second, the growing research literature on coping and stress moved practitioners away from an emphasis on vulnerability and risk and moved them toward an exploration of the ways people cope with environmental challenges. A vulnerability and risk perspective leads practitioners to search for the multitude of factors impinging upon the individual that, in a seemingly unalterable manner, put them at risk for behavioral deviance (Hawkins et al., 1992; Wyman et al., 1993). A resiliency perspective shifts the attitude from fatalism to opportunity. It focuses on finding, enhancing, and encouraging the utilization of coping skills with which to navigate troubled waters.

Finally, practitioners have increasingly grown disillusioned with the usefulness of the traditional clinical disease model that leaned toward an exploration of pathology, injury, victimization, and learned helplessness. An increasing need began to be felt to find hope in the midst of excessive stress and adversity (Rutter, 1987), to focus on wellness and self-repair rather than problems and maladjustment (Wolin and Wolin, 1993).

Different questions began to be framed. The attempt to understand the process by which young people succeed, despite the adversity they face, began to take center stage (Jessor, 1993). Instead of asking what puts youngsters at greater jeopardy of behavioral deviance (for example, substance abuse), the question became: Given similar high risk environments and individual vulnerabilities, why do some people escape relatively unharmed and sometimes strengthened (Kumpfer, 1993). What factors and processes enable sustained competent functioning even in the presence of major life stressors? Equally as important, can we utilize such understanding to strengthen already damaged individuals?

We are indeed talking here about resiliency and resiliency enhancement.

CONCEPTUALIZATION OF THE RESILIENCY PROCESS

Models of the resiliency process differ in some ways, but they all include the interaction of two types of components. First, biological, psychological, and environmental adverse conditions or stressful life events *(risk factors)* have the potential to increase the vulnerability of the individual. Second, personal, family, social, and institutional buffers or supports *(protective factors)* moderate the disruptive potential of individual vulnerabilities and environmental hazards (Jessor, 1993; Kumpfer, 1993; Masten et al., 1990; Rutter, 1989).

Anthony (1987) attempted to explain the components of the resiliency process with the following story. Three dolls, one made of glass, one of plastic, and one of steel, are exposed to the same risk, a heavy hammer blow. The first doll shatters totally. The second sustains a permanent dent. The third responds only with a loud metallic sound. The story is meant to illustrate that like the dolls, individuals have differing capacities to withstand adversity (i.e., differing *vulnerabilities*). They have differing abilities to bounce back to normal, or even better than normal, functioning after a "temporary collapse" precipitated by adversity (i.e., differing *resiliency*). The degree of protection afforded by their environments are important elements in the final outcome (i.e., differing protective factors).

Karol Kumpfer (1993) has proposed a consolidated definitional framework which helps us to understand the resiliency process more clearly. (See Figure 1 below.)

Figure 1
KUMPFER'S FRAMEWORK FOR RESILIENCY

External Environment	Internal Self	Result
Protective Factors	Resiliency	Adaptation
↑ <----------------------> ↑	<---------------> ↑	
↓ <----------------------> ↓	<---------------> ↓	
Risk Factors	Vulnerability	Maladaption

Figure 1 illustrates how qualities of the environment are separate from individual qualities. According to Kumpfer, negative characteristics of the environment should be defined as risk factors, positive characteristics of the environment as protective factors, negative characteristics of the individual should be seen as vulnerability factors, and positive characteristics of the individual as resiliency factors. All interact in the adaptation or maladaptation of the individual, adaptive or competent outcome being the non-abuse of substances and maladaptive or incompetent outcome being the abuse of them.

SOME NOTABLE CONSIDERATIONS ABOUT THE PROCESS

Resilient or adaptive outcome is a process of interaction between individual and environmental factors. It is not a trait or fixed attribute within an individual (Kumpfer,1993; Richardson et al., 1990; Rutter 1989).

Resilient or adaptive outcome is not continuous over time. If circumstances change, the outcome may be different (Luthar, 1991; Rutter, 1989).

Risk and vulnerability factors often co-occur, with additive and possibly exponential negative power. The greater the number of such factors stressing an individual, the greater the likelihood of maladaption and the lesser the likelihood of resilient adaptation (Cowen et al., 1990; Garmezy, 1985; Masten et al., 1990; Rutter, 1979; Werner, 1990).

Almost all of the research studies on resilient individuals that we are about to discuss measured competency or adaptive behavior by observable, behavioral criteria. Resiliency definitely infers behavioral competence, such as non-abuse of substances. However, it is extremely important to note that it may, or may not, include good emotional health. At least one study has found that despite competence on behavioral indices adolescents from high-stress backgrounds had significantly higher scores on depression and anxiety than equally competent adolescents from low-stress backgrounds (Luthar, 1991). And another study found that many behaviorally resilient concentration camp survivors were clearly emotionally troubled (Moskowitz, 1983).

Research efforts to date have focused primarily on determining protective environmental factors and resilient characteristics of high-risk but well-adapted individuals. The results can be categorized into three main areas: a) psychological and/or dispositional attributes of the child; b) affectional ties, cohesiveness and socialization practices within the family; and c) external support systems that reinforce competence and provide a positive value-set for youngsters (Werner, 1990). This chapter will review the research related to the first of these. The next chapter will specifically discuss family and community factors related to resilience.

RESEARCH REVIEW OF INDIVIDUAL FACTORS RELATED TO RESILIENCY

For at least the past four decades researchers have been conducting a large number of studies of particular aspects of resiliency in persons living under extremely stressful conditions. The most famous of these research efforts includes Emmy Werner and Ruth Smith's thirty-year longitudinal study of the entire multi-racial cohort of children born on the island of Kauai, Hawaii, in 1955 (Werner and Smith, 1982, 1992); Project Competence at the University of Minnesota led by Norman Garmezy and his colleagues, which studied resiliency in children of mentally ill parents (Garmezy, 1985); and Michael Rutter's British study of resilience in children at risk because of substantial family dysfunction (Rutter, 1985).

Other important efforts include The Child Resilience Project at the University of Rochester that investigated stress-resistent and stress-affected nine- to twelve-year-olds (Cowen et al., 1990; Wyman et al., 1993); the St. Louis Risk Research Project, which looked at resilience in children of mentally ill parents (Beardslee and Podorefsky, 1988; Worland et al., 1987); and a large number of other studies which looked at resilience in children coping with considerable stress such as inner-city youngsters living in poverty (Clark, 1991; Garmezy, 1991; Luthar, 1991); children from alcoholic families (Berlin and Davis, 1989); concentration camp survivors (Moskowitz, 1983); youngsters coping with diabetes (Hauser et al., 1989; Schwartz et al., 1989); survivors of childhood cancer (Beardslee, 1989); and street children from Colombia (Felsman, 1989).

As a result of these studies a common core of personality characteristics and dispositions has been identified that enable highly stressed children to maintain a sense of control and competence in their lives.

Biological Factors

Two factors that have consistently emerged in the research

77

literature as associated with resiliency are most likely genetically based and as such are not likely to be responsive to intervention: a) easy-going temperament and/or disposition, and b) intellectual capacity.

An easy-going temperament and/or disposition from birth has been identified in several studies as associated with resiliency (Garmezy, 1985; Rutter, 1979; Werner, 1990; Wyman et al., 1993). Werner and Smith (1982) attempt to explain that relationship by suggesting that pleasant, responsive, easy-going individuals tend to elicit more positive responses from persons around them and possibly receive greater support as a result.

Intellectual ability (most importantly, verbal and communication skill) has emerged in several studies as related to resiliency (Garmezy, 1985; Masten et al., 1990; Worland et al., 1987). Such abilities are generally an index of academic aptitude. As such they likely protect youngsters, particularly disadvantaged youth, through their association with academic achievement (Masten et al., 1990).

The relationship between intelligence and resilience is complicated, however. Some studies have indicated the possibility that high intelligence, which is frequently coupled with greater sensitivity to surrounding people and things and therefore greater susceptibility to being overwhelmed, may operate at times as a vulnerability rather than a resiliency factor (Luthar and Zigler, 1991; Masten, 1982).

Personality Factors

Self-efficacy
The one personality characteristic that is most consistently associated with resilient outcome is a sense of self-efficacy. This is a multidimensional trait. It includes a positive perception of one's competence to perform certain tasks (Bandura, 1977); "a feeling of your own worth, as well as a feeling that you can deal with things. That you can control what happens to you." (Rutter, 1984); a "sense of coherence" derived from confidence that one's external and internal worlds are predictable and hopeful, that life makes sense and that one has some control over one's fate—things will work out and odds can be surmounted (Werner, 1985).

Self-efficacy is closely allied to, but not identical with, the concept of internal locus of control. Actually internal locus of control is one aspect of self-efficacy. It is, as Werner and Smith (1982) note, the belief that even in the face of adversity, one can exert considerable control over one's fate. It is the belief that one has some influence over the current environment and one's future destiny (Kumpfer, 1993). The important dimension here that is associated with resiliency is the sense of mastery, the sense of personal power, the feeling that one possesses the potential for command over one's self and one's external environment.

The link between resiliency and self-efficacy has been demonstrated in many studies. Werner and Smith's (1992) resilient Hawaiian youngsters had more faith in their ability to control their environment positively than did the non-resilient participants in the same study. This was also true of Michael Rutter's (1984) high-risk English subjects and Norman Garmezy's (1985) children of mentally ill parents. In both cases the more resilient children felt a greater degree of control over their environment and were more likely to hold the belief that effort pays off. Nine- to twelve-year-old stress-resistent youngsters in the University of Rochester studies were found to have greater self-esteem and a greater sense of competence than their stress-vulnerable age mates (Cowen et al., 1990). Use of alcohol and other drugs was also less likely among those with a greater estimate of their own self-worth and high internal locus of control (Wyman et al., 1993). High self-esteem, a positive self-concept, and a sense of personal power also marked the resilient adolescents with diabetes researched by Schwartz and his colleagues (Schwartz et al., 1989).

Action and belief, some studies suggest, are related to each other. Hays and Ellickson (1990) found adolescents more likely to resist drugs if they previously noted that they believed they would be able to do so. They called this "resistance self-efficacy." The successful pre-teenage street children in Colombia were found by Felsman (1989) to constantly corroborate their belief in their own self-efficacy through effective repeated daily behavior that gained them a livelihood in the streets.

By now it should be apparent that the popular concept of "learned helplessness" (Seligman, 1975), which refers to a state in which the external environment is seen as random and immutable, not within one's personal influence (Luthar and Zigler, 1991; Kumpfer, 1993), is the antithesis of self-efficacy. As we have discussed, self-efficacy has several related components: a sense of self-esteem and self-confidence, a belief in one's ability to have some influence on one's internal and external environment, a sense of personal power. Two other resiliency factors reinforce a sense of self-efficacy. They are the ability to appraise the environment realistically and a repertoire of social problem-solving skills which positively reinforces one's continuing sense of confidence and mastery.

Realistic Appraisal of the Environment

The ability to differentiate between the possible and the impossible is another trait of the resilient individual. Resilient persons are better able to realistically appraise their own abilities and to be cognizant of what they can and cannot do or change. Beardslee and Podorefsky (1988) found in their study of children of parents with affective disorders and children who were cancer survivors that the better-adapted individuals were characterized by their ability to make accurate appraisals of the stress that had to be dealt with and of their own capacity to act and to affect the situation. Stress-resilient pre-teens were found to have greater realistic control attributions than their stress-vulnerable age mates in the research done by Cowen and his Rochester colleagues (Cowen et al., 1990). Garmezy and Masten (1986) and Werner (1986) had similar findings.

Social Problem-Solving Skills

Having a repertoire of social problem-solving skills that serve to enhance one's sense of competency and self-esteem has also been related to resiliency according to many studies, most notably those done in Minnesota, Hawaii, and England. (Masten et al., 1990; Rutter, 1979; Werner and Smith, 1982). Many successful school-based alcohol and other drug abuse prevention programs discussed in Chapter Three recognize the value of social problem-solving skills and include them in their student training (Botvin et al., 1984; Ellickson, 1984; Pentz et al., 1989).

Empathy

The capacity to understand and respond to another's feelings, usually known as empathy, has been identified in a number of studies as a resiliency factor. Both male and female resilient adolescents in Hawaii possessed what is often considered a traditionally feminine characteristic. That is, they were more appreciative, gentle, nurturing, and socially aware than their non-resilient cohort members, possessing a caring and responsible attitude toward others (Werner, 1985; 1987). Stress-resilient pre-teens studied at Rochester had greater empathy than the stress-vulnerable children in the same sample (Cowen et al., 1990). Resilient diabetic youngsters studied by Schwartz and colleagues (1989) had greater interpersonal sensitivity and responsiveness.

The relationship between empathy and resiliency, as with intelligence and resiliency, is somewhat complicated. High empathy may be a vulnerability factor under high-stress conditions. Wyman and colleagues (1993) studied the relationship between the degree of empathy in nine- to twelve-year-olds and their risk of taking drugs. Youngsters with high empathy and low stress were at low risk for drug taking behavior. However, youngsters with high empathy and high stress had a sharply increased risk for such behavior. Under high stress conditions the heightened sensitivity that goes along with high empathy, as with high intelligence, may act as an overload, rather than as a stabilizing, mechanism.

Humor

Several studies have clearly revealed a relationship between humor and resilience. Highly stressed but competent children in the University of Minnesota Project Competence study demonstrated more ability to generate humor than their highly stressed but less-competent counterparts (Garmezy et al., 1984). The highly stressed but capable and resilient ten- to fourteen-year-olds in Masten's (1982, 1986) research revealed greater ability to use humor, appreciated humor more, and were more readily able to find the comic in the tragic and to use humor to reduce tension and restore perspective. According to Kumpfer (1993) such abilities also serve the added function of maintaining social relationships.

Sense of Direction or Mission

About twenty years ago the psychiatrist M. Bleuler reasoned that stressful life events need not have an abnormal outcome if the individual develops some sense of purpose or life task through them (Bleuler, 1978). The resiliency research done since then supports his claim. A number of the children in Moskowitz's study of concentration camp survivors were assigned by their parents and other adults to care for their younger siblings. Most reported that as a result of their single-minded focus on seeing that their younger relatives survived, they, too, survived (Moskowitz, 1983). Similar findings have been reported in a study of civil rights' workers who found strength in fighting for others (Beardslee, 1989); and one of Hawaiian youngsters who had a strong sense of responsibility

81

for helping and taking care of others (Werner & Smith, 1982). In each case, through acts of what might be called "required helpfulness," their lives took on meaning (Garmezy, 1985).

A sense of meaning, of mission, of purpose; a belief in a compelling future can also be sparked by a special talent, a fervent intellectual passion, a strong faith, or a unique interest (Cameron-Bandler, 1986; Danziger and Farber, 1990; Richardson et al., 1990).

Adaptive Distancing

The ability to adopt a healthy separation from the maladaptive patterns of parents and other significant adults has been shown in several studies to serve resilient children well. Faced with alcoholic or drug addicted parents, parents who are mentally ill, or family dysfunction of other types, many youngsters have used this mechanism of adaptive distancing to keep themselves from becoming enmeshed in, and repeating, harmful family patterns. The resilient children did not identify with their dysfunctional relatives, they found successful role models elsewhere. Their ability to think and act separately from the troubled adults and to see themselves as apart from the illness system and not responsible for it marked the healthy coping mechanism of the resilient child. Such youngsters can distinguish between their own experience and their parents' illness. They are saddened by the adults' problems but not overwhelmed by them. Their approach is compassionate but detached (Anthony, 1987; Beardslee, 1989; Beardslee and Podorefsky, 1988).

For children of alcoholics adaptive distancing is a very important safety mechanism. Those who could psychologically step back from their dysfunctional environment adapted best (Anthony 1974; Berlin and Davis, 1989; Berlin et al., 1988; Chess, 1989; Wallerstein, 1983).

At times, adaptive distancing has been mistaken for "reactive distancing," which is best described by flight, fight, and isolation. The former is a condition where separateness and self-understanding prevail. The adaptively distant individuals clearly locate themselves as separate from the ill parent, not as the cause of nor the blame for the illness (Kumpfer, 1993).

A cautionary note needs to be made about this resiliency factor. The rationalization and intellectualization necessary to maintain this position can make it hard for the child to maintain other relationships with adequate levels of intimacy and generativity (Worland et al., 1987).

Gender

Resiliency and gender have been shown to be related in at least three areas: developmental stage, family ecology, and sex-role behavioral expectations.

Developmental Stage

Several studies have found boys to be less resilient than girls in early childhood, while the reverse is true in adolescence. In the first decade of life, cultural sex-role expectations related to control of emotions and aggressive behavior and a paucity of time spent with same sex exemplars put boys at a disadvantage psychologically, socially, and academically (Masten et al., 1990; Rutter, 1989; Werner and Smith, 1982). In the second decade, girls become more vulnerable. Sexual pressures, biological changes, and societal expectations "to be ladylike" in adolescence begin to disadvantage girls. Autonomy and mastery are no longer expected of girls (Benard, 1991; Gilligan et al., 1990). Aggressiveness tends to get boys in trouble in childhood; dependency becomes a major problem for girls in adolescence (Werner and Smith, 1982).

Family Ecology

Boys and girls thrive in somewhat different household environments. Resilient girls in Werner and Smith's (1982) Hawaiian study were most likely to come from households that emphasized risk-taking and independence, where parental overprotection was absent, where reliable support from a primary caretaker was available, and where mothers had long-term employment and fathers were permanently absent (due to death, divorce, or separation). Resilient boys were most likely to come from households with greater structure, rules, and parental supervision; encouragement of emotional responsiveness; and a positive male role model.

Sex-Role Behavior

For both males and females in the Werner and Smith (1982) study, resiliency was related to the adoption of an androgynous personality. The most resilient youngsters blended both masculine and feminine characteristics and acted in a flexible non-sex-typed manner. Youngsters of both sexes were yielding and assertive, expressive and instrumental, able to care about themselves and others. The resilient girls were more autonomous and independent than non-resilient girls. The resilient boys were more emotionally expressive and nurturant than non-resilient boys. Their families encouraged and facilitated this androgynous adaptation.

PROGRAMS DESIGNED TO INCREASE RESILIENCY

Advocates of a resiliency perspective have devoted themselves throughout the last several decades to defining concepts, establishing theory, and completing research. As the focus in the prevention field begins to shift from risk and remediation to one of protection and prevention as a consequence of that work, practitioners are beginning to take the next step and develop programs aimed at resiliency enhancement. Although each project works with different populations, and emphasizes distinctive resiliency factors, each attempts to address at least one of the following four logical enhancement strategies suggested by Ann S. Masten (1994): a) reduce vulnerability and risk; b) reduce exposure to adversity; c) increase available resources; and/or d) mobilize protective processes. A short list of examples are noted below.

William Beardslee and his colleagues at the Judge Baker Children's Center and Harvard Medical School (Beardslee et al., 1992; Steinbaum, 1993) are piloting a program which promotes "adaptive distancing" by encouraging children to see themselves as "separate" from their mentally ill parents.

Emory Cowen and his colleagues at the University of Rochester (Cowen et al., 1990) have developed a curriculum which among other things is aimed at helping children to understand and express feelings, including empathy, to enhance their problem-solving skills, and to cultivate a realistic locus of control.

Roger Mills and his associates' Modello/Homestead Gardens Program in Florida (Mills, 1991, 1992) helps participants to recondition their thinking so as to bring forth a more positive belief system about their own ability to change their life circumstances.

The Rockville, Maryland, Office of Substance Abuse has developed the "Athletes Coaching Teens" Project, which encourages teens to turn their "dreams" into personal goals and develop strategies to reach those goals (Farrell et al., 1992).

These four projects and several others which will be described in the next two chapters are only a small part of the many resiliency enhancement efforts throughout the country.

CONCLUSION

In the past decade there has been increased interest in the concept of resilience—the remarkable capacity of individuals to withstand considerable hardship, to bounce back in the face of great adversity, and to go on to live relatively normal lives. This interest has resulted in a paradigm shift on the part of prevention theoreticians, researchers, and practitioners from a reactive stance that stressed risk management to a proactive stance that stresses resiliency. The substance-abuse prevention field has begun to incorporate this paradigm shift and to look for ways to transfer the knowledge gained into substance-abuse prevention efforts.

Resiliency research has focused on determining protective environmental factors and characteristics of high-risk but well-adapted individuals. This chapter has been concerned with the latter, that is, the dispositional attributes of the child associated with resiliency. The following chapter will discuss the environmental factors, which includes the affectional ties, cohesiveness, and socialization practices within the family associated with resiliency and the external support systems that reinforce competence and provide a positive value-set for youngsters.

Further work, as always, still needs to be done. There are at least three areas that this author finds intriguing. Research that has been done so far has isolated factors associated with resiliency but has not identified the mechanisms at work in reducing risk and promoting protection. We could benefit from knowing not only what factors are associated with resiliency but how and why that is so. Without such knowledge the effective promotion of competence is limited, and the development of interventions to promote resiliency is decidedly handicapped (Rutter, 1994).

Likewise, little work has been done comparing the vulnerability and resilience of adolescents from different racial, cultural, and economic groups. There seems to be a popular assumption that minority-group youngsters, economically impoverished youngsters, and recent immigrants are at greater risk for behavioral deviance such as alcohol and other drug abuse. There is evidence to suggest that for African-American youngsters at least, this is not so (Nettles and Pleck, 1994; Taylor, 1994). Similar work could beneficially be done with other minority groups as well.

Finally, evidence in this chapter suggests that the more androgynous and the less sex stereotyped a youngster is, the more resilient he or she is. The most resilient youngsters come from households that encourage such androgynous adaptation. Few prevention programs building on this theme have yet been developed. Such an approach holds promise for future program development.

For too long substance-abuse prevention programs have been mainly devoted to lessening pathology and risk. A change in focus to resiliency enhancement has shifted the emphasis to strength-building and empowerment. To be comprehensive and realistic prevention programming needs to include both. The challenge of the future is to mobilize the creativity and resources to do just that.

REFERENCES

Anthony, E. J. (1974). The syndrome of the psychologically invulnerable child. In E. J. Anthony and C. Koupernik (Eds.), *The Child in His Family: Children at Psychiatric Risk.* New York: Wiley, 529-545.

Anthony, E.J. (1987). Children at high risk for psychosis growing up successfully. In E.J. Anthony and B.J. Cohler (Eds.), *The Invulnerable Child.* New York: Guilford Press, 147-184.

Bandura, A. (1977). *Social Learning Theory.* Englewood Cliffs, N.J.: Prentice Hall.

Beardslee, W.R. (1989). The role of self-understanding in resilient individuals: The development of a perspective. *The American Journal of Orthopsychiatry, 59(2),* April, 266-278.

Beardslee, W. R., Hoke, L., Wheelock, I., Rothberg, P., Van de Velde, P., and Swatling, S. (1992). Initial findings on preventive intervention for families with parental affective disorders. *American Journal of Psychiatry, 149(10),* 1335-1340.

Beardslee, W.R., and Podorefsky, D. (1988). Resilient adolescents whose parents have serious affective and other psychiatric disorders: Importance of self-understanding and relationships. *American Journal of Psychiatry, 145,* 63-69.

Benard, B. (1991). Fostering resiliency in kids: Protective factors in the family, school and community. Western Regional Center for Drug-Free Schools and Communities, Far West Laboratory, San Francisco, CA. Unpublished manuscript.

Berlin, R., and Davis, R. (1989). Children from alcoholic families: Vulnerability and resilience. In T. Dugan and R. Coles (Eds.), *The Child in our Times: Studies in the Development of Resiliency.* New York: Brunner/Mazel, 81-105.

Berlin, R., Davis, R., and Orenstein, A. (1988). Adaptive and reactive distancing among adolescents from alcoholic families. *Adolescence, 23(91),* 577-584.

Bleuler, M. (1978). *The schizophrenic disorders.* New Haven, Conn: Yale University Press.

Botvin, G.J., Baker, E., Renick, N., and Filazzola, A. (1984). A cognitive-behavioral approach to substance abuse prevention. *Addictive Behaviors, 9,* 137-147.

Cameron-Bandler, L. (1986). Strategies for creating a compelling future. *Focus on Family and Chemical Dependency,* July/August, 6-7.

Chess, S. (1989). Defying the voice of doom. In T. Dugan and R. Coles (Eds.), *The Child in our Times: Studies in the Development of Resiliency.* New York: Brunner/Mazel, 179-199.

Clark, M. (1991). Social identity, peer relations and academic competence of African-American adolescents. *Education and Urban Society, 24(1),* November, 41-52.

Cowen, E., Wyman, P. Work, W., and Parker, G. (1990). The Rochester Child Resilience Project: Overview and summary of first year findings. *Development and Psychopathology, 2,* 193-212.

Danziger, S., and Farber, N. (1990). Keeping inner-city youth in school: Critical experiences of young black women. *Social Work Research and Abstracts, 26(4),* 32-39.

Dryfoos, J. (1990). *Adolescents at Risk: Prevalence and Prevention.* New York: Oxford Press.

Ellickson, P.L. (1984). *Project ALERT: A smoking and drug prevention experiment.* The RAND Corporation, N-2184-CHF: Santa Monica, Calif.

Farrell, A., Howard, C., Danish, S., Smith, A., Mash, J., and Stovall, K. (1992). Athletes coaching teens for substance abuse prevention: Alcohol and other drug use and risk factor in urban middle school students. In C. Marcus and J. Swisher (Eds.), *Working with Youth in High-Risk Environments: Experiences in Prevention.* OSAP Prevention monograph-12. Rockville, Md.

Felsman, J.K. (1989). Risk and resilience in childhood: The lives of street children. In T. Dugan and R. Coles (Eds.), *The Child in Our Times: Studies in the Development of Resiliency*. New York: Brunner/Mazel, 56-79.

Garmezy, N. (1985). Stress-resistant children: The search for protective factors. In J.E. Stevenson (Ed.), Recent Research in Developmental Psychopathology. *Journal of Child Psychology and Psychiatry (Book Suppl. No. 4)*, Oxford: Pergamon Press, 213-233.

Garmezy, N. (1987). Stress, competence and development: Continuities in the study of schizophrenic adults, children vulnerable to psychopathology and the search for stress resistant children. *American Journal of Orthopsychiatry, 57(2)*, 159-174.

Garmezy, N. (1991). Resiliency and vulnerability to adverse developmental outcomes associated with poverty. *American Behavioral Scientist, 34(4)*, 416-430.

Garmezy, N., and Masten, A.S. (1986). Stress, competence, and resilience: Common frontiers for therapist and psychopathologist. *Behavior Therapy, 57(2)*, 159-174.

Garmezy, N., Masten, A.S., and Tellegan, A. (1984). The study of stress and competence in children: A building block for developmental psychopathology. *Child Development, 55,* 97-111.

Gilligan, C., Lyons, N.P., and Hanmer, T.J. (Eds.). (1990). *Making Connections: The Relational Worlds of Adolescent Girls at Emma Willard School.* Cambridge, MA: Harvard University Press.

Hauser, S. T., Vieyra, M. A., Jacobson, A., and Wertlieb, D. (1989). Family aspects of vulnerability and resilience in adolescence: A theoretical perspective. In T. Dugan and R. Coles (Eds.), *The Child in Our Times: Studies in the Development of Resiliency.* New York: Brunner/Mazel, 109-133.

Hawkins, J. D., Catalano, R. F., and Miller, J. Y. (1992). Risk and protective factors for alcohol and other drug problems in adolescence and early adulthood: Implications for substance abuse prevention. *Psychological Bulletin, 112(1),* 64-105.

Hays, R.D., and Ellickson, P.L. (1990). How generalizable are adolescent beliefs about pro-drug pressures and resistance self-efficacy? *Journal of Applied Social Psychology, 20(4),* 321-340.

Jessor, R. (1993). Successful adolescent development among youth in high-risk settings, *American Psychologist, 48(2),* 117-126.

Kumpfer, K. (1993). Resiliency and AOD use prevention in high risk youth. Unpublished manuscript. (Available from School of Social Work, University of Utah, Salt Lake City, Utah, 84112.)

Luthar, S. (1991). Vulnerability and resilience: A study of high risk adolescence. *Child Development, 62(3),* 600-616.

Luthar, S., and Zigler, E. (1991). Vulnerability and competence: A review of research on resilience in childhood. *American Journal of Orthopsychiatry, 61(1),* 7-22.

Masten, A.S. (1982). Humor and creative thinking in stress-resistant children. University of Minnesota. Unpublished doctoral dissertation.

Masten, A.S. (1986). Humor and competence in school aged children. *Child Development, 57,* 461-473.

Masten, A.S., Best, K.M., and Garmezy, N. (1990). Resilience and development: Contributions from the study of children who overcome adversity. *Development and Psychopathology, 2,* 425-444.

Masten, A.S. (1994). Resilience in individual development: Successful adaptation despite risk and adversity. In M. C. Wang and E. W. Gordon (Eds.), *Educational Resilience in Inner-City America: Challenges and Prospects.* New Jersey: Lawrence Erlbaum Assn., 3-25.

Mills, R. (1991). A new understanding of self: The role of affect, state of mind, self-understanding and intrinsic motivation. *Journal of Experimental Education, 60(19),* 67-81.

Mills, R. (1992). Toward a comprehensive model for prevention: A new foundation for understanding the root causes of drug abuse. From reports presented at the Annual Meeting of the Office for Treatment Improvement-Special Initiative Branch, New Orleans, La., on March 31, 1992 and the State of Florida Dept. of Health and Rehabilitative Services Alcohol and Drug Abuse Program, Tallahassee, Fla. (1991-92).

Moskowitz, S. (1983). *Love Despite Hate.* New York: Schocken Books.

Nettles, S. M., and Pleck, J. H. (1994). Risk, resilience and development: The multiple ecologies of black adolescents in the United States. In R. J. Haggerty, L. R. Sherrod, N. Garmezy, and M. Rutter (Eds.), *Stress, Risk and Resilience in Children and Adolescents: Processes, Mechanisms and Interventions.* Cambridge University Press, 147-181.

Pentz, M.A., Dwyer, J., MacKinnon, D., Flay, B.R., et al. (1989). A multicommunity trial for primary prevention of adolescent drug abuse. *Journal of the American Medical Association, 261(2),* 3259-3266.

Richardson, G., Neiger, B., Jensen, S., and Kumpfer, K. (1990). The resiliency model. *Health Education, 21(6),* 33-39.

Rutter, M. (1979). Protective factors in children's responses to stress and disadvantage. In M. W. Kent and J. Rolf (Eds.), *Primary Prevention of Psychopathology, Vol III: Social Competence in Children.* Hanover, N.H., University Press of New England, 49-74.

Rutter, M. (1984). Resilient children, *Psychology Today,* 57-65.

Rutter, M. (1985). Resilience in the face of adversity: Protective factors and resistance to psychiatric disorder, *British Journal of Psychiatry, 147,* 598-611.

Rutter, M. (1987). Psychosocial resilience and protective mechanisms. *American Journal of Orthopsychiatry, 57(3),* 316-331.

Rutter, M. (1989). Psychosocial resilience and protective mechanisms. In E.J. Anthony and B.J. Cohler (Eds.), *The Invulnerable Child.* New York: Guilford Press, 181-21.

Rutter, M. (1994). Stress research: Accomplishments and tasks ahead. In R. J. Haggerty, L. R. Sherrod, N. Garmezy, and M. Rutter (Eds.), *Stress, Risk and Resilience in Children and Adolescents: Processes, Mechanisms and Interventions.* Cambridge University Press, 354-385.

Schwartz, J., Jacobson, A., Hauser, S., and Dornbush, B. (1989). Explorations of vulnerability and resilience: Case studies of diabetic adolescents and their families. In T. Dugan and R. Coles (Eds.), *The Child in Our Times: Studies in the Development of Resiliency.* New York: Brunner/Mazel, 134-144.

Seligman, M. (1975). *Helplessness: On Depression, Development and Death.* San Francisco: Freeman.

Steinbaum, E. (1993). The resilient ones. *Boston Globe*, magazine section, April 25, 10-36.

Taylor, R. D. (1994). Risk and resilience: Contextual influences on the development of African-American adolescents. In M. C. Wang and E. W. Gordon (Eds.), *Educational Resilience in Inner-City America: Challenges and Prospects.* New Jersey: Lawrence Erlbaum Assn., 147-181.

Wallerstein, J. (1983). Children of divorce: Preliminary report of a ten-year follow-up of older children and adolescents. *Journal of the American Academy of Child Psychiatry, 24,* 545-553.

Werner, E. E. (1985). Stress and protective factors in children's lives. In A. R. Nicol (Ed.), *Longitudinal studies in child psychology and psychiatry.* New York: Wiley and Sons, 335-355.

Werner, E. E. (1986). Resilient offspring of alcoholics: A longitudinal study from birth to age 18. *American Journal of Orthopsychiatry, 59,* 72-81.

Werner, E. E. (1987). Vulnerability and resiliency in children at risk for delinquency: A longitudinal study from birth to young adulthood. In J. Burchard and S. Burchard (Eds.), *Prevention of Delinquent Behavior.* Newbury Park: Sage, X, 16-43.

Werner, E. E. (1990). High risk children in young adulthood: A longitudinal study from birth to 32 years. *American Journal of Orthopsychiatry, 59(1),* January, 72-81.

Werner, E. E., and Smith, R. S. (1982). *Vulnerable but Invincible.* New York: McGraw-Hill.

Werner, E. E., and Smith, R. S. (1992). *Overcoming the Odds: High Risk Children from Birth to Adulthood.* Ithaca, N. Y.: Cornell University Press.

Wolin, S.J., and Wolin, S. (1993). *The Resilient Self: How Survivors of Troubled Families Rise Above Adversity.* New York: Villard Books.

Worland, J, Weeks, D., and Janes, C. (1987). Predicting mental health in children at risk. In E. J. Anthony and B. J. Cohler (Eds.), *The Invulnerable Child.* New York: Guilford Press, 185-210.

Wyman, P., Work, W., Hightower, A., and Kerley, J. (1993). *Relationships Among Childhood Competencies, Psychological Stress, and Substance Use Risk Behaviors in Early Adolescence.* New York: Univ. of Rochester. Unpublished manuscript.

CHAPTER 5

Building on Strengths: Risk and Resiliency in the Family, School, and Community

Sandra Turner

INTRODUCTION

Substance abuse prevention researchers and programmers are incorporating resiliency strategies into their work with youngsters. Programs focus on the enhancement of strengths rather than on the elimination of risk factors on the assumption that building positive relationships, reinforcing coping mechanisms, fostering talents and skills, and generally fostering a sense of belonging to family, school, and community will all serve as preventive measures against substance use and misuse (Benard, 1994).

This resiliency paradigm as well as new research on adolescent girls development particularly stresses the importance of significant and consistent positive relationships in the enhancement of inherent and acquired strengths in adolescents. The relationships formed in families, schools, and communities are now found to have a powerful influence on adolescent development in general and, specifically on the development of resiliency (Benard, 1994, Gilligan et al., 1990). This chapter will focus on the building of those relationships as well as the other qualities of families, schools, and communities that contribute to the development and enhancement of resiliency as it relates to the prevention of adolescent substance abuse.

RISK AND RESILIENCY

Risk-focused and resiliency-focused approaches both try to accomplish the same thing—to make youth better able to resist substance misuse. Those who subscribe to a risk-focused approach concentrate on eliminating or lessening the risk factors that a youngster is exposed to. This approach focuses on problems and aims to "fix" or "solve" them before they become more serious (Hawkins et al., 1992).

A resiliency-focused approach, on the other hand, looks at what is right and tries to protect or enhance it. For example, a risk-focused approach to working with a youngster growing up in an alcoholic home might be to try to get the substance abusers into treatment, whereas a resiliency-based approach would support the youngster's ability to detach from the harmful effects of the alcoholic environment.

THEORETICAL FOUNDATION OF RESILIENCY

The work in resiliency builds on Social Learning Theory and Cognitive Behavioral Theory (Bandura, 1977; and Beck, 1976) and incorporates aspects of Health Realization Theory, recently developed by Roger Mills (1991). Social Learning Theory stresses the importance of modeling behavior—that is, that behavior is learned by observing other's behavior as well as by direct experiences. In Cognitive Behavioral Theory, the emphasis is on how a person thinks about him or herself and how he or she cognitively views the world. Cognitive Behaviorists stress the importance of recognizing negative thoughts and then working to change these thoughts as well as the behaviors that flow from them.

Mills' Health Realization Theory resembles both Cognitive Behavioral Theory and Social Learning Theory in that it recognizes the importance of perceptions. Mills believes that everyone has the innate capacity to function with self-esteem and good judgment. Understanding one's own moods and taking actions in a good mood, not in a bad mood, can help engender secure and positive feelings about oneself (Mills, 1991).

Hope is a foundation of resiliency, an attribute which also plays a major role in theories of depression. Seligman (1975, 1990) hypothesizes that what primarily differentiates the depressed from those who are not is a sense of hope or internal, realistic locus of control. People need to see a positive relationship between their own actions and outcomes of these actions.

FAMILY RISK FACTORS

The more risk factors a youngster encounters, the more vulnerable he or she becomes, and the more likely he or she will engage in substance misuse or other problematic behavior (Hawkins et al., 1992). What exactly are the family risk factors that can lead to vulnerability and maladjustment?

1. *Being born into poverty* (Garmezy, 1991, Hawkins et al., 1992).

2. *Chronic familial tension and discord.* Some studies have found that family conflict is a more serious risk factor and therefore a stronger predictor of substance misuse than divorce or separation (Rutter and Giller, 1983).

3. *Having a parent or sibling who abuses alcohol or other drugs.* As Social Learning Theory predicts, adolescents growing up in families where drug use is modeled tend to adopt that behavior. However, it is important to note that while parents and older siblings may use alcohol and other drugs themselves, if they take a firm position of non-use for their children and younger siblings, they can exert a positive influence (Brook et al., 1986).

4. *Parental non-directiveness and permissiveness of any kind.* However, authoritarian parental decision making is not effective unless it is combined with a democratic process of reason and negotiation with the family members (Baumrind, 1983).

5. *The death of a significant adult,* serious or chronic illness (their own or that of their primary caretaker), and divorce or separation of parents (Werner and Smith, 1992, Hauser et al., 1984).

6. *Living in a family in which one or both parents or caretakers are seriously disturbed or dysfunctional,* especially if this results in the inability of the primary caretaker to bond and become involved in a major way in the child's life, (Hawkins et al., 1992).

7. *Suffering physical or sexual abuse as a child or adolescent* (Hauser et al., 1989). The younger the age at which a child experiences any kind of abuse in the family, the more pernicious are the effects (Gomes-Schwartz et al., 1990).

Gender and Ethnic Differences

It is important to note that, just as all stressors do not affect children and adolescents uniformly, some important differences characterize gender and ethnicity. In their studies of resiliency, Werner and Smith (1982, 1992) analyzed gender variations and found significant differences. They found that, in general, boys are more vulnerable in the first decade of life, whereas girls become more vulnerable in the second decade. Boys are affected more by prenatal stress than girls, and they are then more physically vulnerable in infancy and early childhood. Boys who exhibit a combination of shy and aggressive behavior and are thus socially ill at ease, tend to be more emotionally vulnerable at ages four to six (Werner and Smith, 1992).

Also, boys are more affected than girls by separation and loss of parents or primary caretakers in early and middle childhood, while girls are more vulnerable than boys to chronic familial discord and disturbed interpersonal relationships in adolescence. Just as aggressive behavior and lack of social skills can be a problem for boys in childhood, dependency can be a problem for girls in adolescence (Werner and Smith, 1992).

Girls are generally more vulnerable than boys in adolescence, starting at ages eleven and twelve. This is the age when girls often start to do poorly in school and their self-esteem begins to plummet (Gilligan et al., 1990). Girls who experience teenage pregnancies or early marriages are especially unprotected.

Few studies have looked at family risk factors in terms of race, although Garmezy (1991) discussed the role of poverty in the development of risk factors and family stress, and a study done by the Children's Defense Fund found that: "America's Black children were twice as likely as White children to (a) die in the first year, (b) be born prematurely, (c) suffer low birth weight, (d) have mothers who received little or no prenatal care, and (e) have no employed parent" (Garmezy, 1991, p. 415). Almost 50 percent of black children and two-fifths of Hispanic children in America live in poverty.

FAMILY PROTECTIVE FACTORS

Ironically, risk may be a necessary prerequisite for resiliency. It is perhaps the falling apart or disruption caused by several severe life stressors that impels a person to look inward and adapt—to learn new skills which will enhance his or her ability to adapt and hurdle life events (Richardson et al., 1990). Werner and Smith (1992) found that the more stressors a person was exposed to, the more protective factors were needed to offset these stressors to help enhance resiliency.

The family still exerts the most influence over the child's emotional, social, psychological, and physical environment. This is true whether one is raised by two parents, a single parent, other kin, or foster parents. There are many protective factors, which help to build resiliency, that the family can instill. What follows are some of the most important family protective factors.

1. *Biological or Genetic Factors*. The building of family protective factors begins before the birth of the child with the provision of quality prenatal care for the mother (Werner and Smith, 1982, 1992). Babies who have not suffered prenatal stress and who have a heavier birth weight are more likely to have more regular sleep patterns, to be calmer, and to have a good ability to self-soothe (Werner and Smith, 1992). Babies exposed to alcohol and other drugs in the womb are more likely to suffer birth defects and other problems such as mental retardation, hyperactivity and agitation, withdrawal symptoms, low birth weight, and difficulty in self-soothing. As discussed earlier, poverty is a major risk factor at any age, and the risks to the child begin before birth, since poor women often have difficulty obtaining good prenatal care, a problem compounded if they are also drug abusers (Chavkin, 1990). Benard (1993) talks about creating a continuum of caring as we work to build resiliency. Provision of good prenatal care is an essential first step in the development of family protective factors.

2. *Warm, Positive Relationship with a Caring Adult*. According to Staggers (1991) the majority of the adolescents surveyed felt that the single most important thing for them was to spend time with an adult who cares about them. Other prevention researchers have also found that having a warm, positive long-term relationship with an adult caretaker may be the most important family protective factor for young children and adolescents (Rutter, 1979, Kumpfer, 1993, Werner, 1987). Rutter (1979) and Wolin and Wolin (1993) found that having a warm and supportive relationship with at least one person (parent, coach, or other consistent and positive adult) can offset the negative influence of a dysfunctional parent. Nettles (1993) has found the coaching relationship to be a powerful one. Coaches, not only for athletics but for all kinds of activities, can provide a structured learning environment for the development of competence and self-esteem.

3. *Positive Family Environment and Bonding*. Cohesive, supportive families offer protection even when there is also dysfunction, such as parental substance abuse (Kumpfer and DeMarsh, 1985). Brook et al., (1986) found that children who are attached to their parents and involved in family activities, whatever they may be, are less likely to initiate substance use. Parents help build resiliency if they are involved in and supportive of a child's developing talents,

competencies, and life choices (school, friends, courses, clothes, part-time jobs). A family or friend or teacher involved in a positive way in a child's decision-making process, especially at key turning points in his or her life, will help build self-esteem and self-efficacy (Rutter, 1979).

4. *Family Responsibilities*. Werner (1982, 1992) concluded that it is important for children to have responsibilities in their homes. Parents who assign chores on a regular basis help to build resiliency. Bleuler (1978) also found that youngsters who know that their families are counting on them to do certain tasks on a regular basis will feel valued and significant. High-risk youth who are given responsibility for taking care of some aspect of family functioning such as caring for a younger sibling, taking charge of pets, or cleaning will internalize a feeling of competence and a sense that they can be counted on.

5. *High Parental Expectations*. Parents who have high, but realistic, expectations for their children will enhance their resiliency (Kumpfer and DeMarsh, 1985). Parents who convey a message to their children of belief in their competence will help them internalize an optimistic attitude about their abilities (Mills, 1991, Benard, 1994). Knowing that someone else believes in you helps people believe in themselves.

6. *Extended Family Support Networks*. Garmezy (1993) has documented the importance of extended family support systems. The contemporary nuclear family has in many ways cut itself off from extended family and friend support, but resilient families are aware of the protective nature of this kind of support system (Garmezy, 1993).

Werner (1979) also found how important extended family and friends who become like family can be. Referred to by some as "Mother Resilience," Werner recently stated that one factor that she attributes to her own resilience is the fact that she has kept her friends since kindergarten (Benard, 1995). A mother who has other adults who can be counted on to help with child rearing is more able to maintain emotional stability and feelings of warmth toward her children (Werner and Smith, 1982). This argues for the development of support systems of uncles, aunts, roommates, close friends, etc. for the benefit of both the primary caretaker and her or his children. We have long known of the value of grandparents, particularly if they are not assuming primary responsibility for the care of children, as a tremendous source of nurturing and loving support.

7. *Family Traditions and Rituals*. Wolin and Wolin (1993), who have done extensive work with children growing up in alcoholic families, have found that firm family rituals and traditions in the midst of great dysfunction will serve as powerful mitigating forces. Children who can count on always having Sunday dinner together, or having holidays or birthdays celebrated, or visiting Grandma on a regular basis will internalize a sense of family cohesion. Being able to depend on regular family rituals and traditions helps youngsters internalize a routine and a sense of predictability around which they can build a sense of personal freedom (Wolin and Wolin, 1993). This helps them feel freer to come and go if they know there is something to come back to when they want to.

8. *Positive Parental Modeling—Good Parenting Skills*. Parents who model resilient behavior will convey the message to their children that they can learn to behave in similar ways. Social Learning Theory posits behavior is learned from watching and modeling the behavior of others (Bandura, 1977). Many prevention programs teach parenting skills or family effectiveness training and are finding this to be an effective prevention strategy, particularly in combination with parental involvement in school policy and resistance skills training (Johnson et al., 1989). As with the establishment of family rituals, even parents who are dysfunctional themselves, in terms of substance use, can be coached to develop more effective parenting styles (Kumpfer and DeMarsh, 1985). If they can be helped to establish good communication patterns and firm family boundaries and to respect their adolescents' individuality while providing consistent supervision and discipline, they will lay a protective foundation.

Firm parental discipline and consistently enforced rules in an atmosphere of praise and support are extremely important, especially for adolescents (Werner and Smith, 1982, Hauser et al., 1989). Baumrind (1991) found that authoritative but democratic parents who developed clear and reliable family policies tended to produce the most competent resilient youth. Lewis (1991) has also found that simply using powerful control techniques is often ineffective and that encouraging verbal give and take, using reason and negotiation, and being willing to comply with some of their children's requests are more successful.

Different Protective Factors for Boys and Girls

Girls who are perceived as "cuddly" derive protection from this factor in childhood, while for boys it is positive to be perceived as "active" (Werner and Smith, 1992). Girls whose mothers work outside the home, particularly in jobs they find fulfilling, tend to be more resilient, whereas boys' resiliency is enhanced by having a male mentor and being the first born son.

Masten (1991) found that for both boys and girls those who had more androgynous characteristics were the most resilient. These findings are similar to those of Bem (1993), who has studied the psychological benefits for both men and women of being androgynous.

Feminist scholars are finding that it is positive for girls to develop resistant strategies or qualities. Resistance in this context is seen as a healthy quality or psychological strength that enables girls to "resist" a hostile environment of negative messages (Gilligan et al., 1990, Schultz, 1990). Feminist researchers advocate that adolescent girls begin to speak honestly and openly about their lives. This form of resistance can be frightening for adolescent girls as it may cut them loose form the conventional security of the "traditional quiet female" (Brown, 1992). To be able to tell their own life stories, adolescent girls need support and encouragement and strong female role models who are also telling their own stories honestly and boldly. Scholars of color argue against "racelessness" that is the strategy for minimizing cultural connections in order to be accepted in a white world. Feminist scholars are disavowing "genderlessness" and calling for women to speak as women and affirm their connections to each other and their unique experiences and points of view (Robinson and Ward, 1991).

Racial Protective Factors

Some scholars make a distinction between "resistance for survival and resistance for liberation" and encourage women in general and women of color in particular to move beyond striving for individual survival in a sometimes hostile and oppressive world. Robinson and Ward (1991) advocate transcending this kind of "quick fix" solution and moving to practicing resistance for liberation. This kind of resistance draws upon the strengths of one's history and cultural connections.

Nettles (1993) has investigated the effect of race in terms of risk and protection and found that, for adolescent blacks, growing up and going to school with whites can serve as a protective factor.

SCHOOL PROTECTIVE FACTORS

Although the family may be the single most influential buffering factor in childhood and later adaptation, the outside environment—school, peers, and community—is also extremely important. Schools have always exerted great influence on adolescent development and life choices, and as school days become longer with the institution of before-school breakfasts and after-school programs that can last until 6 P.M. for children of working mothers, the influence of the school will become even greater. Some researchers and educators are advocating school restructuring to change to an outcome-based educational approach that facilitates all students learning well (Towers, 1992). Schools can cultivate resiliency in the following ways.

1. *Opportunities for Involvement in School Climate Decisions*. Schools that create an environment of caring, cooperation, and student involvement will help to develop resiliency. Schools that are incorporating a restructuring approach have expanded opportunities for student and parental involvement, have high expectations for achievement of their students, have child-centered activity learning, and integrated instructional approaches (Spady, 1988). Students feel more competent and valued if they have a "say" in school policy. One public school in New York City recently reactivated a long-defunct student council and began an after-school program run by both parent volunteers and paid staff. There was an enthusiastic response to both of these initiatives: many students joined both programs, more students started wearing the school tee shirts, those who chose to join were regarded as leaders, and there seemed to be a general feeling of increased pride in the school (P.S. 3 parent). As a result of staff cutbacks, many teachers have started using parent volunteers in their classes. This parent was recently asked to help with conflict resolution between several third-grade girls, and the results were very positive.

Positive involvement in school in any number of ways (athletic, artistic, musical, vocational, organizational) is just as important in building competency as academic success. Many people have emphasized the human need to bond—to belong and to have a feeling of control over one's life. Schools that are able to instill this sense of belonging effectively enhance resiliency. Schools that promote a school identity where children of all races perceive the environment as supportive do a lot to combat racism (Nettles, 1993).

2. *High Expectations for Student's Performance.* Schools that convey an attitude of high but realistic expectations for all of their students will produce more successful graduates (Benard, 1992). Mills (1991) believes that everyone has access to a higher self, and that parents, teachers, and siblings or peers who have high but realistic expectations give a message of "you can do it!" Schools that mainstream special education youth and develop programs such as reading recovery without stigma are creating an atmosphere of possibility and high expectations for all.

Schools that initiate partnerships with community businesses are also showing successful results (Spady, 1988). One New York City elementary school recently initiated a reading program with volunteers from a nearby large advertising agency who devote their lunch time to serving as reading coaches to first through fifth graders.

3. *Caring, Supportive Atmosphere.* Programs in which students are encouraged to teach each other are successful. Programs where sixth graders tutor third graders on a regular basis are showing positive results. The older children serve as role models, and all the youth are given help on a regular basis. Teachers who use more cooperative learning groups and peer tutoring foster mutual support and increase learning opportunities, again without stigma. In this way, youth who need more academic help get it in a positive atmosphere. Youngsters serve as compelling role models for each other, and those who are taught to help each other will create an atmosphere where resiliency can grow. It is also important that the teachers and other staff in school convey a message of caring and concern. If students feel their teachers care about them and want to spend time with them, they will feel they are worthwhile. Teachers can serve as positive role models and confidants as well as instructors of academic skills.

Alice Goldberger was a teacher who ran a school in London for children of Nazi concentration camp victims (Moskowitz, 1983). Most of these children grew up into resilient adults. When they were interviewed in their adulthood, they remembered their teacher as the greatest influence on their lives. It was she who provided the love, kindness, and compassion which they had been deprived of. She also taught them to be compassionate even though they had not been treated compassionately in their early lives.

COMMUNITY PROTECTIVE FACTORS

Prevention researchers are finding that the ways in which various community institutions interact with each other to produce clear and consistent messages and opportunities for youth have a critical effect on their social and educational development (Ianni, 1993). Communities can be defined in different ways, by geographic location, school, business, religion, ethnic group, or politics. No matter how they are defined, they provide the context for the functioning of families, schools and peer groups. Some prominent researchers in the field of resiliency believe that it is the responsibility of state and national governments to provide community services for children and families who are in environments of risk (Garmezy, 1991). Some believe that the provision of community protective services are national and state responsibilities. Services such as child care, nutrition and health care programs, and recreational resources are all examples of community services that help build resiliency.

1. *Positive Community Norms.* Communities where there is a sense of belonging, caring, commitment, and mutual protection, and non- drug use norms are likely to foster resiliency in their youth. By the third grade youngsters know if they are in the mainstream or out of it, and if they perceive themselves as out of the mainstream of society, they have much less incentive to act in pro-social ways, not to take drugs (Finnegan, 1990). Although anti-social in their activities, street gangs provide a powerful sense of support and belonging for their members. If communities could provide this same sense of support and belonging in a pro-social and positive way, the effect would be tremendous. Benard (1992) calls for a partnership of parents, schools, and community institutions that fosters behavior that is pro-social and urges these partners to move beyond risks and "actively engage children and develop their competencies" (Benard, 1992, p. 7).

Communities where there are ever-present advertisements selling cigarettes or alcohol give a message to youth that this is what the community finds acceptable and desirable. One recent study found that by age three, one-third of the children in the U.S. know who "Old Joe Cool Camel" is, and that by age six, 90 percent of American children associate him with cigarettes in general and Camel cigarettes, in particular (Hall and Zigler, 1992). In general ads on T.V. and billboards continue to glamorize the use of cigarettes and alcohol, and this has a potent effect on youth, especially preadolescents and adolescents. The media give youth the message that they should primarily be consumers. A community that can counter-balance this message will serve a vital protective function.

2. *Community Resources for Parents and Children*. Quality schools, recreational opportunities, health care, housing, child care, job training, and employment are all basic resources needed for the development of resilient children. Many researchers agree that community provision of these resources is a major protective factor for high risk youth.

3. *Community Bonding*. As has been discussed social bonding is a major protective mechanism. Community bonding is made up of family bonding, school and peer bonding, and bonding to religious and community institutions such as community centers, businesses, sports centers, community recycling centers or neighborhood parks and libraries.

CONCLUSION

The shift in focus from risk to resiliency in the field of substance misuse prevention represents a shift from programs that "do things to kids" to programs that demand active participation of "kids," parents, schools, and communities (Duncan, 1994). It also focuses on strengths and protective factors rather than risk factors. A recent evaluation of one of the largest school-based prevention programs in the U.S. found that this program, based on risk-factor prevention, has been largely ineffective. Youth reported that they felt judged rather than supported by the prevention program personnel (Benard, 1995). While it is possible to identify students who may be at risk, it is very difficult to provide the individualized services that may benefit these students. A strengths—or resiliency—based perspective builds on the thriving aspects of all the students.

Prevention researchers and program developers are now calling for the development of partnerships among families, schools, and communities to create a responsive environment to meet the basic needs of youth and foster the development of essential competencies. Resilient youngsters are those whose families, schools, and communities have joined together with them to help build problem-solving skills, a sense of hope, purpose and belonging, and a belief in themselves and in their own abilities (Duncan, 1994). Scholars and program developers working within the resiliency framework believe it is essential to view young people as resources with whom to work to create a shared vision of strength and competency (Loftquist, 1992).

REFERENCES

Bandura, A. (1977). *Social Learning Theory*. Englewood Cliffs, NJ: Prentice Hall.

Baumrind, D. (1983, October). Why adolescents take chances—And why they don't. Paper presented at the National Institute for Child Health and Human Development, Bethesda, MD.

Baumrind, D. (1991). The influence of parenting style on adolescent competence and substance use. *Journal of Early Adolescence, 11(1)*, 56-95.

Beck, A. (1976). *Cognitive Therapy and the Emotional Disorders*. New York: International Universities Press.

Bem, S. L. (1993). *The Lenses of Gender*. New Haven, CT: Yale University Press.

Benard, B. (1990). *The Case for Peers*. Portland, OR: Western Center for Drug-Free Schools and Communities.

Benard, B. (1992). How schools convey high expectations for kids. *Western Center News, 5(3)*. Portland, OR: Northwest Regional Educational Laboratory, Western Regional Center for Drug-Free Schools and Communities.

Benard, B. (April 1993). Discussion during conference on "Putting Resiliency into Substance Abuse Prevention for Adolescents." Unpublished presentation, New York.

Benard, B. (1994). Guides for the journey from risk to resilience. *Western Center News, 7(4)*. Portland, OR: Northwest Regional Educational Laboratory, Western Regional Center for Drug-Free Schools and Communities.

Benard, B. (1995). Interview with Emmy Werner, "Mother Resilience". *Western Center News, 8(2)*. Portland, OR: Northwest Regional Educational Laboratory, Western Regional Center for Drug-Free Schools and Communities.

Benard, B. (1995). Statewide evaluation finds need for new focus. *Western Center News, 8(3)*. Portland, OR: Northwest Regional Educational Laboratory, Western Regional Center for Drug-Free Schools and Communities.

Bleuler, M. (1978). *The Schizophrenic Disorders*. New Haven, CT: Yale University Press.

Brook, J., Gordon, A.S., Whiteman, M., and Cohen, P. (1986). Some models and mechanisms for explaining the impact of maternal and adolescent characteristics on adolescent stage of drug use. *Developmental Psychology, 22*, 460-467.

Brown, L.M. (1992). A problem of vision: The development of voice and relational knowledge in girls ages 7-16. Unpublished manuscript.

Chavkin, W. (July 10, 1990). Help, don't fail addicted mothers. *Village Voice*, p. 11.

Duncan, A. (1994). Resiliency concept offers best chance for change. *Western Center News, 8(1)*. Portland, OR: Northwest Regional Educational Laboratory. Western Center for Drug-Free Schools and Communities.

Finnegan, W. (1990). Drug dealing in New Haven, part I. *The New Yorker*. September 17.

Garmezy, N. (1991). Resiliency and vulnerability to adverse developmental outcomes associated with poverty. *The American Behavioral Scientist, 34(4)*, 416-430.

Garmezy, N. (April 1993). Discussion during conference on "Putting Resiliency into Substance Abuse Prevention for Adolescents." Unpublished presentation, New York.

Gilligan, C., Lyons, N.P., and Hanmer, T.J. (Eds.). (1990). *Making Connections: The Relational Worlds of Adolescent Girls at Emma Willard School*. Cambridge, MA: Harvard University Press.

Gomes-Schwartz, B., Horowitz, J., and Cardarell, A. (1990). *Child Sexual Abuse: The Initial Effects*. Newbury Park, CA: Sage.

Hall, N., and Zigler, E. (1992). *Substance Abuse Prevention: A Review Relevant to Pre-school Interventions - Theory, Practice and Programs*. Yale University Bush Center of Child Development and Social Policy.

Hauser, S.T., Powers, S.I., Noam, G.G., and Jacobson, A. (1984). Familial contexts of adolescent ego development. *Child Development, 55*, 195-213.

Hauser, S.T., Vieyra, M.A., Jacobson, A., and Wertlieb, D. (1989). Familial contexts of adolescent ego development. *Child Development, 55*, 195-213.

Hawkins, J.D., Catalano, R.F., and Miller, J.Y. (1992). Risk and protective factors for alcohol and other drug problems in adolescence and early adulthood: Implications for substance abuse prevention. *Psychological Bulletin, 112(1)*, 64-105.

Ianni, F. (1993). *Joining Youth Needs and Program Services*. Urban Diversity Series No. 104. New York: ERIC Clearinghouse on Urban Education.

Johnson, C.A., Pentz, M.A., Weber, M.D., Dwyer, J.H., MacKinnon, D.P., Flay, B., Baer, N.A., and Hansen, W.B. (1989). The relative effectiveness of comprehensive community programming for drug abuse with high-risk and low-risk adolescents. *Journal of Consulting and Clinical Psychology, 588(4)*, 447-456.

Kumpfer, K. (1993). Resiliency and AOD use prevention in high risk youth. Unpublished manuscript. Available from School of Social Work, University of Utah, Salt Lake City, UT 84112.

Kumpfer, K., and DeMarsh, J. (1985). Family environmental and genetic influences on children's future chemical dependency. *Journal of Children in Contemporary Society: Advances in Theory and Applied Research, 18*, 49-92.

Lewis, C.S. (1991). The effects of parental firm control: A reinterpretation of findings. *Psychological Bulletin, 90(3)*, 547-563.

Loftquist, W. (1992). Let's create a new culture of youth work in America. *New Designs for Youth Development*, p. 23-27.

Masten, A. (1991, November). Risk and resilience in children. Paper presented at the Protecting Vulnerable Children Project, Children of Alcoholics Foundation, Inc., Princeton University, Princeton, New Jersey.

Mills, R. (1991). A new understanding of self: The role of affect, state of mind, self-understanding and intrinsic motivation. *Journal of Experimental Education, 60(10)*, 67-81.

Moskowitz, S. (1983). *Love Despite Hate*. New York: Schocken Books.

Nettles, S. M. (April 1993). Discussion during conference on "Putting Resiliency into Substance Abuse Prevention for Adolescents." Unpublished presentation, New York.

Richardson, G.E., Neiger, B.L., Jensen, S., and Kumpfer, K. (1990). The resiliency model. *Health Education, 21(6)*, 33-39.

Robinson, R., and Ward, J.V. (1991). "A belief in self far greater than anyone's disbelief": Cultivating resistance among African American female adolescents. In C. Gilligan, A. Rogers, and D. Tolman (Eds.), *Women, Girls & Psychotherapy: Reframing Resistance*. New York: Haworth Press.

Rutter, M. (1979). Protective factors in children's responses to stress and disadvantage, In N.W. Kent and J. Rolf (Eds.), *Primary Prevention of Psychopathology: Vol. 3. Social Competence in Children*, pp. 49-74. Hanover, NH: University Press of New England.

Rutter, M., and Giller, H. (1983). *Juvenile Delinquency: Trends and Perspectives*. New York: Penguin.

111

Schultz, D. (1990). *Risk, Resiliency, and Resistance: Current Research on Adolescent Girls*. New York: National Council for Research on Women.

Seligman, M. (1975). *Helplessness: On Depression, Development and Death*. San Francisco: Freeman.

Seligman, M. (1990). *Learned Optimism: How to Change Your Mind and Your Life*. New York: Simon and Schuster.

Spady, W.J. (1988). Organizing for results: the basis of authentic restructuring and reform. *Educational Leadership, 46(2)*, 4-8.

Staggers, B. (November 1991). Discussion during Conference for Prevention Specialists, Oakland, CA. Unpublished presentation.

Towers, J.M. (1992). Outcome-based education: another educational bandwagon? *Educational Forum, 56(3)*, 291-305.

Werner, E. (1979). The transactional model: Application to the longitudinal study of the high risk child on the Island of Kauai, Hawaii. Paper presented at the Biannual Meeting of the Society for Research on Child Development, San Francisco.

Werner, E. (1987). Vulnerability and resiliency in children at risk for delinquency: A longitudinal study from birth to young adulthood. In J. Burchard and S. Burchard (Eds.), *Prevention of Delinquent Behavior*, pp. 16-43. Newbury Park, CA: Sage.

Werner, E., and Smith, R.S. (1982). *Vulnerable but Invincible*. New York: McGraw-Hill.

Werner, E., and Smith, R.S. (1992). *Overcoming the Odds: High Risk Children from Birth to Adulthood*. Ithaca, NY: Cornell University Press.

Wolin, S., and Wolin, S. (1993). *The Resilient Self*. New York: Villard Books.

CHAPTER 6

Resilience in African American Adolescents: Issues Pertinent to Alcohol and Other Substance Use

Saundra Murray Nettles

The resilience construct is a popular one as evident in numerous reviews of an expanding conceptual and research base (see, for examples, reviews by Masten et al., 1990 and volumes edited by Wang and Gordon, 1994; and Haggerty et al., 1994) and in use of the construct to undergird prevention efforts (Gardner et al., 1994). In this chapter, which addresses use of alcohol, tobacco, and other drugs (ATOD) by African American youths, resilience refers to abstinence, experimentation, or occasional use over time. Maladaptive outcomes consist of frequent usage or abuse, or usage that leads to other behavioral, psychosocial, or physical dysfunctions.

Policy makers and researchers interested in African American children and youth have welcomed the burgeoning interest in studies of resilience with ambivalence. The research focus on individuals who succeed despite exposure to risk is encouraging after years of theoretical and empirical perspectives that highlight deficits (Winfield, 1991). Yet, some argue that emphasis on individuals who succeed despite adversity will undermine public support for social solutions to problem behavior that results in teen pregnancy, delinquency, school drop out and ATOD abuse (Nettles and Pleck, 1994). Others comment that the resilience construct is in need of further clarification (Gordon and Song, 1994). These reservations suggest the need for further attention to questions of *how* the resilience process works to create sustained coping in populations at risk for ATOD abuse and other risky behavior (Gordon and Song, 1994; Hawkins et al., 1992; Masten, 1994). Without such attention, we are limited in our ability to tap the full potential of the resilience construct for application to prevention programs for ATOD abuse and other problem behaviors.

This chapter considers programmatic strategies and conceptual models of successful adaptation as they apply to African American youth. The first section presents a brief overview of the extent of ATOD use among African American adolescents. This is followed by discussions of risk and protective factors, respectively. Models of the resilience process are the topics of the next section, and the last major section addresses African-centered models for African American youths.

INCIDENCE AND CONSEQUENCES OF ATOD USE AMONG AFRICAN AMERICAN ADOLESCENTS

Enduring images of black youths engaged in alcohol and other drug-related activity are brought to us constantly by the media and everyday conversation in the workplace, schools, and homes. Yet, the data reveal a different picture. As reviewed by Nettles and Pleck (1994) national surveys based upon self-reports consistently indicate that African American youths use alcohol and "soft" drugs (e.g., marijuana) marginally less often than white, Native American, and Hispanic youths (see also Dryfoos, 1990; D.C. Gottfredson et al., 1995; Singleton, 1989). For example, in the 1990 National Household Survey on Drug Use 10.8 percent of black males in the twelve to seventeen age group reported that they used marijuana in the last year; 12.2 percent of the white males in that age group reported that they used marijuana in the last year. Self-reported alcohol use for the same age group was 16.1 percent in the last month and 28.7 percent in the last month for African American and white males, respectively. Among females, marijuana use in the last month was 7.8 percent and 11.8 percent for blacks and whites aged twelve to seventeen; and for alcohol use, the rates were 14.6 percent and 27.3 percent for blacks and whites, respectively. Use of cocaine is very low for all groups, but it is lowest for black youths. There are no significant racial/ethnic differences in use of hard drugs (Dryfoos, 1990).

However, the period between adolescence and early adulthood is one of increased vulnerability (i.e., the individual's susceptibility to an adverse consequence) for blacks, whose risk for abuse of alcohol and soft drugs increases substantially (Lowman et al., 1983, cited in Goddard, 1993; National Institute on Drug Abuse, 1991). Moreover, black youth experience greater adverse consequences from substance use than other groups. Such consequences include alcohol-related disorders and cocaine-related admissions to emergency rooms (Nettles and Pleck, 1994). For example, although there are 80 percent fewer black than white males, young black males are equally likely to be admitted to emergency rooms for cocaine-related episodes (National Center for Health Statistics, 1991).

Amuleru-Marshall (1993) attributes these differences to social injustice:

> These patterned differentials in mortality, morbidity, and incarceration are indicative of an unjust social order, that is, one characterized by political and economic injustice. Their relationship to AOD abuse is not merely an indirect one. The major causes of black avoidable mortality and hospitalization are directly associated with tobacco, alcohol, and other drug use and addiction, while the overwhelming majority of incarcerated individuals in this country have AOD involvement histories (p. 25).

Data from reports of drug arrests and drug-related hospital admissions, which show that young black males have the highest rates of all groups, suggest that African American youths underreport drug use in national surveys. As reviewed by Nettles and Pleck (1994), Mensh and Kandel (1988) found that black youths were significantly more likely to say that they had never used marijuana in one national survey when they had previously reported in another survey that they had. Yet another study (Cox et al., 1992) found inconsistencies between blacks and whites to be only slight in responses on national surveys.

These methodological issues notwithstanding, young and low-income populations living in inner cities confront multiple risks for ATOD abuse associated with poverty of the social area and the greater presence of licit and illicit drugs in the community. In addition to area socioeconomic status being a risk factor for ATOD, many other risk factors for drug abuse have been identified. These factors are examined in the next section.

RISK FACTORS

Risk factors are characteristics of groups that are associated with heightened negative outcomes for the group in question. For individuals within these populations, risk status, or exposure to risk must be determined. D.C. Gottfredson and colleagues (1995) reviewed the literature to determine the empirical basis for risk factors that have been identified in the research and intervention literature. This review presented risk factors for ATOD or other problem behaviors (i.e., delinquency, school failure, and risky sexual behavior) that co-occur, or overlap, with ATOD. Because one of the purposes of the review was to document the psychometric properties of instruments for diverse populations, the demographic make-up of study samples was identified. For nearly all of the risk factors identified for white samples, consistent findings were obtained for African American children and youths. The factors are shown below, grouped according to the three categories used in the review:

1. *community environment and organization*: actual availability of substances, perceived availability of substances, formal laws and policies (e.g., taxes on alcohol, age restrictions), low attachment to community.

2. *family environment and family-related activities*: parental attitudes favorable to use; family conflict; parental monitoring, supervision, and consistency of discipline; low support from family and low attachment to family.

3. *individual characteristics, experiences, behaviors, and attitudes*: ATOD use at an early age, attachment and commitment to school and work, academic failure experiences, exposure to negative peers, early problem behavior, religiosity (negative correlate), attitudes favoring drug use, low belief in conventional rules, low self-efficacy.

Note that self-esteem and external locus of control, two factors widely believed to put African American youths at risk for ATOD, are not among the factors identified in the review. Hawkins et al. (1992) identified additional factors, namely, those that were biochemical and genetic. Hawkins and colleagues further note that a greater risk of ATOD use is associated with a greater number of risk factors present.

PROTECTIVE FACTORS

Protective factors and resilience are the positive counterparts to risk factors and vulnerability (Werner, 1990). Protective factors for ATOD are those that inhibit use, and they are important to consider in preventive strategies because some risk factors are not alterable by intervention.

Many investigators have defined protective factors as simply the opposite ends of the dimensions defining risk factors. This is illustrated in a study (Denver Youth Survey et al., 1993) that found that parental supervision, attachment to parents, and consistency of parental discipline are important factors that protect African American, white, and Latino youths in risky environments. Also important were commitment to school and avoidance of peers who use drugs or are delinquent. These factors are the opposite ends of dimensions defining the risk factors named in the section above.

As reviewed by Nettles and Pleck (1994) protective factors for African American youth for other problem behaviors (i.e., teen pregnancy, academic failure, and delinquency) fell into the general categories consistently identified in other research, namely individual factors, family factors, and support from persons in the environment (Garmezy, 1991). For example, religious belief or affiliation with a religious community is associated with educational attainment and competence for both African American and white youth (Brown and Gary, 1991; Masten et al., 1990).

In studies that examined differences within groups of African American youth, protective factors that emerged included race pride (Spencer, 1987), biculturality (i.e., use of skills that permit active participation in African American and mainstream culture), and raceless identity, that is, an identity that encompasses a denial of institutional racism, lack of identification with other African Americans, and behavior reflecting mainstream values. Active parental support for education and closeness to friends who value achievement were also important protective factors for both groups. However, factors protective in one context (such as having bicultural skills in the school environment) may not be in others (Clark, 1991). There is some anecdotal and research evidence that mentors serve protective functions for both groups as well (Flaxman et al., 1988; Freedman, 1988; McPartland and Nettles, 1991).

Alternative conceptualizations specify protective mechanisms rather than factors that facilitate good outcomes (resilience) in individuals who are exposed to risk (Garmezy et al., 1984; Hawkins et al., 1992; Rutter, 1987). Little research has addressed protection for ATOD use defined in this way, although some studies of social competence indicate that the skills associated with the construct are protective (The Consortium on the School-based Promotion of Social Competence, 1994).

MODELS OF THE RESILIENCE PROCESS

The conceptualization of resilience presented in the overview above and in the two preceding chapters in this book included four components: 1) risk factors or vulnerabilities; 2) protective factors as characteristics of the individual; 3) protective factors in the environment (e.g., the family); and 4) the nature of the adversity or stressors (i.e., ATOD use) faced by the individual. Other components include the developmental path of the young person and the context for adaptation (Masten, 1994).

Models of resilience specify *how* resilience occurs—that is, the nature of causal relationships among the various components that lead to successful adaptation. Models are useful because they focus attention on relationships that might be the basis for future development or refinement of interventions.

Three process models of resilience are described below: the multicultural model of the stress process (Slavin et al., 1991), the academic resilience model (Connell et al., 1994), and the developmental model of risk-taking behavior (Levitt et al., 1991). The models are pertinent to African American youth, but their use does not preclude application with other groups.

The Multicultural Model of Stress and Coping

The multicultural model of the stress process recognizes the relevance of culture. According to this conceptual model, culturally-relevant dimensions play a role at every stage, namely, exposure to stress, appraisal of the stressful event, coping, and adaptation. For example, when stressful events occur, they may be related to racial discrimination or socioeconomic status of the individual. Further, cultural and family definitions about a stressful event are presumed to influence the primary appraisal that the individual makes ("Am I in trouble?"), and ethnic identity and beliefs about the ethnic group's efficacy are hypothesized to influence secondary appraisal ("What's to be done about this?"). Coping efforts (both problem focused and emotion focused) are the hypothesized actions in the multicultural model. Coping is also presumed to be culturally relevant (e.g., the individual with a bicultural identity may have the skills to negotiate in minority and majority settings). The choice of coping efforts is directed toward adaptive outcomes—social functioning, morale, and somatic health—that are also culturally defined (Slavin et al., 1991).

The Academic Resilience Model

The academic resilience model has been validated in three separate samples of African American young adolescents living in high-risk environments. These environments include neighborhood risk (such as socioeconomic status, joblessness, and residential stability) and family economic risk. Four components comprise the model: 1) context, i.e., perceived parental involvement; 2) self (or meaning-making processes); 3) action (school-related engagement); and 4) academic-related outcomes. According to the model, students' perceived parental involvement is one of the interpersonal contexts the students experience within the high risk environment. Student perceptions of parental involvement influence processes relating to self-appraisal, i.e., general self concept, efficacy in school, and perceived quality of interpersonal relationships. These self processes influence emotional engagement (e.g., satisfaction with school) and behavioral engagement (e.g., doing homework). Depending on the level of engagement, negative (e.g., low grades) or positive (e.g., high attendance) outcomes are possible. Also, engagement affects parental involvement.

For a detailed discussion of the validation of this general model and its theoretical origins, the reader is referred to Connell et al., (1994).

The Developmental Model of Risk-Taking

The developmental model of risk-taking specifically addresses resilience as it applies to prevention of ATOD abuse and other problem behaviors. Thus two of its components, knowledge and social influence skills (risk management skills), refer to commonly used prevention strategies. For example, knowledge encompasses facts and information that children and adolescents receive in schools and other environments about the risks and consequences of ATOD use. The interventions, geared to the student's developmental level, take place within a risk environment comprised of two sets of risk factors: 1) biologically-based personal dispositions (such as temperament) and 2) the socio-cultural environment, consisting of peers, family, and community contexts.

Knowledge and risk management skills are hypothesized to be filtered through a psychosocial component, the personal meaning (attitudes, values, and beliefs) that the risky situation has for the developing young person. Personal meaning coordinates 1) knowledge and management skills the student has at an abstract level, with 2) the student's own investment in issues related to the risky behavior. Moreover, the developmental levels of the components are presumed to coincide (i.e., they are synchronous). The outcomes are presumed to be risk-related behaviors and choices that are functionally adaptive (Levitt et al., 1991).

Summary

The above models of resilience can be interpreted as recognizing that resilience takes place within specific *risk environments*, or *contexts*, that include for example, neighborhoods, the family, and the peer group. All of the models explicitly define environments in terms of risk factors or stressors, although the definitions could be extended to include protective processes as well. Further, in these models the individual actively considers the *meaning* attached to the risk environment, his or her options for action, and the possible consequences of that action. In short, the concept of meaning in these three models includes issues in which the person is likely to have a personal investment. The models specify some form of *action*, which can draw on the protective elements of the person's skills, knowledge, and affect. The results of these actions are adaptive (resilient) or maladaptive *outcomes*.

Implications for Research and Practice

The risk environment. In drug prevention efforts, most attention has been centered on the risk environment. Reducing vulnerability and risk is the strategy underlying primary prevention. Programs are therefore ained at eliminating or minimizing exposure to risk. According to Hawkins (1992) two approaches predominate, 1) supply manipulation, interdiction and enforcement, and 2) altering social norms. The latter category includes interventions such as media campaigns against drug use and classroom based skills training. An example of such a risk reduction strategy is Project LEAD:High Expectations, a community- and resiliency-based program that is delivered by The Links Foundation, Inc. for African American adolescents and young adults. The program offers core courses, among others, on self-image, values, decision making, and prevention of ATOD use (Gardner et al., 1994).

Another approach to altering the risk environment has been early intervention to reduce risk and pileup of stressors (Masten, 1994; Rutter, 1987). Research has consistently confirmed that poor African Americans, as well as other impoverished groups, face numerous risks to development that begin at birth and continue through childhood and adolescence (Natriello et al., 1990). Many of these risks (such as academic failure experiences) are also risk factors for substance abuse. Several reviews and handbooks address this strategy in detail (see Masten, 1994; Meisels and Shonkoff, 1990)

Increasing available resources is a third approach to risk reduction (Masten, 1994). This strategy calls for making services, people, materials, and other resources available to at-risk youth. An example of this strategy in ATOD abuse prevention is the school-based clinic. In the evaluation of the use of this method in clinics in cities in six states, Kirby et al. (1989) examined alcohol and tobacco consumption at four sites. Compared to schools without clinics, three of the clinic sites reported lower alcohol use, and one clinic reported a lower rate of cigarette smoking.

Several aspects of prevention for African Americans emerge from the discussion above. First, there is a need to identify and address important developmental transitions at which intervention might be particularly critical. For African American students, the transition to third grade has been cited as one such point that is particularly risky. During this transition, depressed levels of academic performance, one of the risk factors for ATOD use, and other problem behaviors often are evident. As noted in the section on incidence and consequences of ATOD use, another crucial point seems to be the transition from adolescence to early adulthood. Intervention must prepare those at risk by providing opportunities and resources needed for them to complete important transitions with a minimum of adverse consequences.

Second, there is a need for good assessment. Despite the plethora of programs available for African American youths, rigorous evaluations of these programs to reduce risk are sparse. For programs without adequate funding for evaluation, several self-study guides to evaluation are available (see, for example, Bain and Herman, 1989; G.D. Gottfredson et al., 1994). D.C. Gottfredson and colleagues (1995) are completing a compendium of instruments suitable for measuring risk factors and program outcomes in diverse populations.

Third, environmental protective processes against ATOD abuse need to be identified in research and practice—mobilizing protective resources is one of the key strategies for fostering resilience (Masten, 1994). For practical purposes, prevention specialists can note, in program applications and intake forms, the sources of support in the family and other contexts (such as a teacher in the school and a coach or mentor in the neighborhood) already available. Social support has emerged consistently as a protective process in studies of persons who have coped successfully with adversity (Nettles, 1991). Also it is important to assess participants' actual exposure to risk as well as protective factors within the youth (for example, bicultural coping skills) so that resilience as a program outcome can be determined.

Meaning and action. The models of resilience suggest ways to deliver resources in meaningful ways to black youths. One way is to reconsider prevention programs as contexts for fostering meaning. This might lead to a more detailed analysis of various roles and tasks that staff undertake. These analyses of tasks can serve as tools for supervisors and evaluators and for answering questions such as: Why does program success depend so much on a "good" staff? What are the specific interactions in which staff and participants engage? How does multicultural content and service delivery contribute to personal meaning?

A second idea implied by the models is that information on the quality of youths' experiences need to be addressed in contexts in which alcohol and other drugs are used. Such information could address questions such as the following: How does the racial mix of the social setting influence ATOD use? With what expectations do African American adolescents go to social activities? To get drunk? To relieve boredom? To feel relaxed enough to take sexual risks? Such information could inform our understanding about the meaning of risk-taking for youths at all levels of risk and illuminate the processes and mechanisms underlying each of the components of resilience models.

A third idea suggests the need for increased understanding on the role of African-centered content and service delivery in fostering meaning and decision making in risky situations for African-American youths. Below, we briefly address that topic.

Are Other Models Needed for African American Youth?

The resiliency-based model of ATOD use is but one of many models that are being applied to drug-related behavior of black youth. As reviewed by Singleton (1989), other models fall into three categories: 1) conventional models of adolescent substance use, including the widely accepted problem behavior theory; 2) models with black adolescents, including, among others, the antisocial behavior model; and 3) alternative models, which reject attention to deficit approaches in categories one and two, in favor of approaches that emphasize the unique cultural, historical, and current circumstances of African Americans.

One alternative model is the African-centered model of prevention for African American youth at high risk (Nobles and Goddard, 1993). This model describes a process to promote healthy development; it is explicitly focused on fostering resilience, among other outcomes. The five key components of the model are:

1. *cultural precepts* (e.g., interdependence and cooperation), which are the philosophical tenets underlying the model

2. *intent*, the aims toward which program activities are focused, including development of a sense of competence and commitment

3. *content*, the domain of knowledge and skills that program activities should encompass, namely African and African-American culture, history, values, skills, and virtues

4. *process*, which refers to the methods (such as culturally consistent problem solving) used to make the content meaningful to the Black adolescent

5. *objectives and outcomes* in the domains of knowledge, attitudes, beliefs, and behavior.

The model goes beyond a resiliency-based approach. It stipulates the socialization of black youths within an Afro-centric, rather than mainstream, community. The culture, structure, and processes within the African American community are redefined, in alignment with an African, rather than European, perspective. Further, the model is intended to address the deep sense of alienation that black youth experience as evident in the high rates of drug-related behavior in the community. As reviewed by Morris (1993), the Hawk Federation Manhood and Development Training Program, developed by Nobles and Goddard, is being assessed for its usefulness as a preventive program for ATOD use and other problems.

Another model is incorporated into the Rites of Passage Project implemented by the West Dallas Community Centers. This project is Afrocentric in that African history, culture, and world views comprise the program content, and program processes include intergenerational involvement, reeducation, and training of participants and assistance to families by intensive-care teams. The content areas include family history, spiritual/community spirit, African American history and culture, time management/organization skills, and sex education among others.

As with ATOD programs for African American youths that are based on resilience and other mainstream models, evidence for the effectiveness of African-centered programs is sparse.

CONCLUSION

The overview of risk factors indicated that, when risk outcomes are considered, African American youth appear to be less at risk than other populations. However, when usage of alcohol and soft drugs is considered, young black males are more at risk for drug-related emergency room admissions and arrest rates than other groups. Data such as these have lead some to suggest that the environment for black adolescents in inner cities is so risky that issues regarding prevention should be formulated differently for African Americans. The African-centered conceptual models of ATOD use and prevention programs based on these models are in response to these concerns.

Each of the models discussed herein makes different contributions to our understanding of the resilience process. The multicultural model reminds us that cultural dimensions can be relevant for each of the components of resilience. The academic and risk-taking models underscore the importance of the context for adaptation, and the risk-taking model emphasizes the need for the developmental level of the person to be considered in prevention practice. All the models highlight the importance of meaning-making by way of appraisal, self-processes, or decision-based attitudes, norms, and values. With the contributions of the African-centered models, these frameworks of resilience point the way toward greater understanding of how resilience can be fostered in African Americans and other youths.

REFERENCES

Amuleru-Marshall, O. (1993). Political and economic implications of alcohol and other drugs in the African-American community. In L.L. Goddard (Ed.), *An African-centered Model of Prevention for American-American Youth at High Risk* (pp. 23-33). Rockville, MD: U.S. Department of Health and Human Services, Center for Substance Abuse Prevention.

Bain, G., and Herman, J.L. (1989). *Improving Opportunities for Underachieving Minority Students: Processes, Mechanisms, and Intervention*. Los Angeles, CA: University of California Center for Research on Evaluation, Standards, and Student Testing.

Brown, D.R., and Gary, L.E. (1991). Religion, socialization, and educational attainment among African Americans: An empirical assessment. *Journal of Negro Education, 60*, 411-426.

Clark, M.L. (1991). Social identity, peer relations, and academic competence of African-American adolescents. *Education and Urban Society, 24*, 41-52.

Connell, J.P., Spencer, M.B., and Aber, J.L. (1994). Educational risk and resilience in African-American youth: Context, self, action, and outcomes in school. *Child Development, 65*, 493-506.

The Consortium for the School-based Promotion of Social Competence. (1994). The school-based promotion of social competence: Theory, research, practice, and policy. In R.J. Haggerty, L.R. Sherrod, N. Garmezy, and M. Rutter (Eds.), *Stress, Risk, and Resilience in Children and Adolescents: Processes, Mechanisms, and Intervention* (pp. 268-316). New York: Cambridge University Press.

Cox, B.G., Witt, M.B., Traccarella, M.A., and Perez-Michael, A.M. (1992). Inconsistent reporting of drug use in 1988. In C.F. Turner. J.T. Lessler, and J.C. Gfroerer (Eds.), *Survey Measurement of Drug Use: Methodological Studies* (pp. 109-154). Rockville, MD: National Institute on Drug Abuse.

Denver Youth Survey, Pittsburgh Youth Study, and Rochester Youth Development Study. (1993). *Urban Delinquency and Substance Abuse: Initial Findings Report.* Washington, DC: U.S. Department of Justice, Office of Juvenile Justice and Delinquency Prevention.

Dryfoos, J.G. (1990). *Adolescents at Risk: Prevalence and Prevention.* New York: Oxford University Press.

Flaxman, E., Ascher, C., and Harrington, C. (1988). *Mentoring Programs and Practices: An Analysis of the Literature.* New York: Teachers College, Institute for Urban and Minority Education.

Freedman, M. (1988). *Partners in Growth: Elder Mentors and At-risk Youth.* Philadelphia: Public Private Ventures.

Gardner, S.E., Green, P.F., and Marcus, J.D. (1994). *Signs of Effectiveness II: Preventing Alcohol, Tobacco, and Other Drug Use: A Risk Factor/Resiliency-based Approach.* Rockville, MD: U.S. Department of Health and Human Services, Center for Substance Abuse Prevention.

Garmezy, N.G. (1991). Resilience in children's adaptation to negative life events and stressed environments. *Pediatric Annals, 20(9),* 459-466.

Garmezy, N., Masten, A., and Tellegen, A. (1984). The study of stress and competence in children: Building blocks for developmental psychopathology. *Child Development, 55,* 97-111.

Goddard, L.L. (1993). Alcohol and other drug abuse literature, 1980-1989: Selected abstracts. In L.L.Goddard (Ed.), *An African-centered Model of Prevention for American-American Youth at High Risk* (pp. 47-56). Rockville, MD: U.S. Department of Health and Human Services, Center for Substance Abuse Prevention.

Gordon, E.W., and Song, L.D. (1994). Variations in the experience of resilience. In M.C. Wang and E.W. Gordon (Eds.), *Educational Resilience in Inner-city America: Challenges and Prospects* (pp. 27-43). Hillsdale, NJ: Lawrence Erlbaum.

Gottfredson, D.C., Harmon, M.A., Gottfredson, G.D., Jones, E.M., and Celestin, J.A. (1995). *Measuring Prevention Outcomes*. Rockville, MD: U.S. Department of Health and Human Services, Center for Substance Abuse Prevention.

Gottfredson, G.D., Nettles, S.M., and McHugh, B.E. (1994). *Program Development and Evaluation for Schools and Communities*. Baltimore, MD: Johns Hopkins Center for Research on Effective Schooling for Disadvantaged Students.

Haggerty, R.J., Sherrod, L.,Garmezy, N., and Rutter, M. (Eds.) (1994). *Stress, Risk, and Resilience in Children and Adolescents: Processes, Mechanisms, and Intervention*. New York: Cambridge University Press.

Hawkins, J.D., Catalano, R.F., and Miller, J.Y. (1992). Risk and protective factors for alcohol and other drug problems in adolescence and early adulthood: Implications for substance abuse prevention. *Psychological Bulletin, 112(1)*, 64-105.

Kirby, D., Waszak, C.S., and Ziegler, J. (1989). *An Assessment of Six School-based Clinics: Services, Impact, and Potential*. Washington, DC: Center for Population Options.

Levitt, M.Z., Selman, R.L., and Richmond, J.B. (1991). The psychosocial foundations of early adolescents' high-risk behavior: Implications for research and practice. *Journal of Research on Adolescence, 1(4)*, 349-378.

Long, L.C. (1993). An Afrocentric intervention strategy. In L.L.Goddard (Ed.), *An African-centered Model of Prevention for American-American Youth at High Risk* (pp. 87-92). Rockville, MD: U.S. Department of Health and Human Services, Center for Substance Abuse Prevention.

Lowman, C., Harford, T., and Kaelberg, C. (1983). Alcohol use among Black senior high school students. *Alcohol Health and Research World, 7(3)*, 37-46.

Masten, A.S. (1994). Resilience in individual development: successful adaptation despite risk and adversity. In M.C. Wang, and E.W. Gordon (Eds.), *Educational Resilience in Inner-city America: Challenges and Prospects* (pp. 3-25). Hillsdale, NJ: Lawrence Erlbaum.

Masten, A.S., Best, K.M., and Garmezy, N. (1990). Resilience and development: Contributions from the study of children who overcame adversity. *Development and Psychopathology, 2*, 425-444.

Meisels, S.J., and Shonkoff, J.P. (Eds.).(1990). *Handbook of early Childhood Intervention*. New York, Cambridge University Press.

Mensh, B.S., and Kandel, D.B. (1988). Underreporting of substance use in a national longitudinal youth cohort. *Public Opinion Quarterly, 52*, 101-124.

McPartland, J., and Nettles, S.M. (1991). Using community adults as advocates or mentors for at-risk middle school students: A two-year evaluation of Project RAISE. *American Journal of Education, 99*, 568-586.

Morris, M. (1993). The complex nature of prevention in the African-American community: The problem of conceptualization. In L.L. Goddard (Ed.), *An African-centered Model of Prevention for American-American Youth at High Risk* (pp. 59-71). Rockville, MD: U.S. Department of Health and Human Services, Center for Substance Abuse Prevention.

National Center for Health Statistics. (1991). *Health, United States, 1990*. Hyattsville, MD: Public Health Service.

National Institute on Drug Abuse. (1991). *National Household Survey on Drug Abuse: Main Findings*. Rockville, MD.

Natriello, G., McDill, E.L., and Pallas, A.M. (1990). *Schooling Disadvantaged Children: Racing Against Catastrophe*. New York: Teachers College Press.

Nelson-LeGall, S., and Jones, E. (1991). Classroom help-seeking behavior of African American children. *Education and Urban Society, 24*, 27-40.

Nettles, S.M. (1991). Community contributions to school outcomes of African American students. *Education and Urban Society, 24*, 132-147.

Nettles, S.M., and Pleck, J.H. (1994). Risk, resilience, development: The multiple ecologies of black adolescents in the United States. In R.J. Haggerty, L.R. Sherrod, N. Garmezy, and M. Rutter (Eds.), *Stress, Risk, and Resilience in Children and Adolescents: Processes, Mechanisms, and Intervention* (pp. 147-181). New York: Cambridge University Press.

Nobles, W.E., and Goddard, L.L. (1993). An African-centered model of prevention for African-American youth at high risk. In L.L. Goddard (Ed.), *An African-centered Model of Prevention for American-American Youth at High Risk* (pp. 115-129). Rockville, MD: U.S. Department of Health and Human Services, Center for Substance Abuse Prevention.

Rutter, M. (1987). Psychosocial resilience and protective mechanisms. *American Journal of Orthopsychiatry, 57*, 316-331.

Singleton, E.G. (1989). Substance use and black youth. In R. Jones (Ed.), *Black Adolescents* (pp. 385-492). Berkeley, CA: Cobb & Henry.

Slavin, L.A., Rainer, K.L., McCreary, M.L., and Gowda, K.K. (1991). Toward a multicultural model of the stress process. *Journal of Counseling & Development, 70*, 156-163.

Spencer, M. (1987). Black children's ethnic identity formation: Risk and resilience of castelike minorities. In J. Phinney and M.J. Rotheram (Eds.), *Children's Ethnic Socialization* (pp. 103-116). Newbury Park, CA: Sage.

Wang, M.C., and Gordon, E.W. (Eds.). (1994). *Educational Resilience in Inner-city America: Challenges and Prospects*. Hillsdale, N.J.: Lawrence Erlbaum.

Werner, E.E. (1990). Protective factors and individual resilience. In S.J. Meisels and J.P. Shonkoff (Eds.), *Handbook of Early Childhood Intervention* (pp. 97-116). New York: Cambridge University Press.

Winfield, L.F.(1991). Resilience, schooling, and development in African-American youth: A conceptual framework. *Education and Urban Society, 24*, 5-14.

CHAPTER 7

Did We Make a Difference?: Techniques and Process in Program Evaluation

Michael Phillips

Many people believe that program evaluations are merely designed to answer the question, "did this program achieve its desired result?" While this is clearly one function, it can have other purposes. You may want the answer to questions such as, "Is this program operating as projected?" "Is this approach to service delivery better than another approach?" "Does this program work equally well with males and females?" While these questions differ from the program's level of success, they are legitimate evaluation questions. Evaluations can be designed to analyze the planning of a project, the structure of a program, the process by which the services are delivered, the success of the program, and the cost benefit of the program. Each of these questions are answered by a different source of data, and a range of research approaches can be used. What all have in common is the use of standardized, replicable procedures to answer the question being posed.

The different evaluation questions are to some degree cumulative. If the evaluator only explores the achievement of the program's goals and doesn't analyze what services are offered and the process by which they are delivered, the researcher will be unable to define what caused the success or failure. Evaluation both justifies a program's usefulness and builds knowledge about what works best.

An evaluation report might state that a given program provided counseling. Without a more complete definition of what is being provided, one does not know whether a cognitive approach, a behavioralist approach, or a psychodynamic approach was used. Even if the model of counseling has been defined, there is the question of what is actually done in counseling sessions and the extent to which those actions actually reflect the model of treatment.

On an even more basic level, there is the question of whether the resources (space, personnel, training, etc.) are in place to implement the service program as projected. Too often a program is defined as a failure even though it never had the resources to put in place the needed program elements. Structural problems may prevent provision of adequate services, which leads to the program not achieving its desired result. In such cases the program was never tested. This chapter will explore the development of evaluation in the context of the three levels of structure, process, and outcome.

Before moving on to the specifics of program evaluation, it is important to make several points: 1) evaluation is always done in a political context; 2) outside evaluators can serve to guard against avoidable bias; and 3) there is considerable value in the evaluator and service provider working together on the development of both the program and the research. The political context involves why the evaluation is being asked for, who is asking for it, why the staff might be willing to share what they do, and what is the researcher's agenda (Weiss, 1975; Suchman, 1967). Weiss has pointed out that programs are created by political decisions, and evaluation reports make a political statement about a program in the way the findings are presented. Further decisions based upon evaluations are sifted through a political process. While evaluation should always be an objective process, only if the evaluators understand the many stakeholder agendas (including their own) can distorted findings be avoided.

USE OF OUTSIDE EVALUATOR

Excellent evaluations can be conducted by administrators, supervisors, and direct service personnel. However, one may want an outside evaluator for a number of reasons. An outside evaluator will question program assumptions regarding structure, process, and outcome, thereby helping to clarify what the program is doing and what it is designed to achieve. An outside evaluator may have better access to computers and statistical packages. An outside evaluator would be familiar with methodological issues that may not have been considered. And finally, decision makers will be more likely to accept findings provided by a "disinterested" party.

Program planners may feel they cannot afford the costs of an outside evaluator yet evaluators may be available at local colleges and universities at little or no cost. University researchers may be willing to work on an evaluation very cheaply because they are interested in the topic, or the research may provide the basis for a professional publication. They may even be able to identify sources of external funding that will pay their fees. Evaluation assistance may also be available from State Departments of Substance Abuse, which may have consultants who can help in designing programs. Federal substance abuse departments like CSAP have consultants who can provide technical assistance and publications that include lists of measurement instruments.

If the outside evaluator and the service provider work together in the development of the program, many problems can be avoided since they can develop a joint understanding about what outcomes the program is to achieve through what input. Thus measures can be designed to tap the outcomes that administrators and service providers are focusing on. Since evaluations depend upon the willingness of staff to share their work, it is extremely important that the staff help define their stake in the evaluation. Staff should help to develop instruments that they feel reflect what they are doing.

FORMULATIVE EVALUATIONS

It is rarely appropriate for a new multifaceted service program to begin by evaluating the impact of the service. The first year should be devoted to conducting a "formulative" evaluation. A formulative evaluation has as its purpose providing quick feedback to program staff about issues and problems that need to be addressed in developing the best possible program. Formulative evaluation provides information on problems of program implementation so they may be addressed in future replications. Formulative evaluations take varying amounts of time, but in new programs they rarely take less than a year. In newly designed multiyear interventions formulative evaluation activities may continue for a number of years. For example, a substance abuse prevention program provided repeated classroom-based programs to the same class in the fourth, fifth, sixth, seven, and eighth grades. Each year a detailed write-up of the class sessions was reviewed by the evaluator to identify what aspects of the program worked well and what was problematic for that age group. On the basis of the review, feedback was provided to staff, who then revised the classroom lessons. The modified lessons were then implemented with a new cohort, and records of the modified approach were reviewed. This is an example of an ongoing formulative evaluation, using a qualitative method, to both investigate the services provided and develop a tested curriculum. By comparing outcomes for the two years, the impact of programmatic changes could be identified.

THE CLASSICAL EXPERIMENT

Evaluations are an effort to create experiments in the real world by approximating the approaches used in a classical experiment. The classical experiment involves:
1. Random selection of subjects.
2. Randomly assigning them to experimental and control groups.
3. Selection of a measurement device that reflects the expected outcome.
4. Measurement of the status of the two groups before the intervention.
5. Control of the type and/or intensity of intervention provided to the experimental group.
6. Measurement of the status of the two groups after the completion of the intervention and
7. Assessment of differences between the experimental and control groups.

This format is designed to assure that the differences between the changes found in the experimental and control group are due to the impact of the intervention and not some extraneous factor. Since in the real world one cannot exercise the same degree of control as in the laboratory, some compromises are made to adjust for the problems one faces. I will briefly discuss those compromises here, going into greater detail later in this chapter.

NEED FOR COMPARISON GROUPS

To "prove" that a program has caused a given change, one needs to compare the results from the intervention cases to some other non-treated group. Without such a comparison, you cannot say whether untreated persons might have changed in a similar way. Two basic types of comparison are possible, a control group or a contrast group. The difference between the two is largely defined by the degree to which one can be sure that the intervention (experimental) and the comparison groups were initially similar. The traditional approach involves random assignment of subjects to intervention and control groups. One begins by drawing a random sample of the population one wishes to study. The term "population" refers to all people meeting a designated set of specifications such as all students in XYZ school. Using a random selection procedure allows one to select a sample that is in all likelihood representative of the larger population.

From this sample one randomly assigns subjects to intervention (experimental) and control groups. By using random assignment it is possible (within the limits of chance) to develop two groups that are considered equivalent prior to the implementation of the intervention. The experimental group then receives the intervention and the control group does not. This ideal procedure is usually not possible because one can rarely assign a sample totally at random. For example, selecting students at random from a school would mean that every class would include both intervention and control children. Arranging times for the intervention would be a scheduling nightmare for the school, and school administrators are unlikely to approve such a plan.

Methods have been developed to approximate randomly assigned experimental and control subjects. One method involves randomly assigning groups, for example whole classes, to the experimental and control groups. A second alternative is to use a contrast group. Contrast groups theoretically are similar in all ways to the experimental group except that they did not receive the intervention. For example, if a program was being provided in one community center one might compare the changes among those children with changes among children in another community center, which has roughly the same population and is situated in a similar socio-economic area. It is not necessary to have a comparison group of the same size as the intervention group though groups should be large enough to reduce errors of measurement. In practice this involves groups of forty or more.

MATCHING

Since it is difficult to find groups that are the same in all respects other than having been exposed to the prevention program, one may attempt to match the experimental and comparison group subjects on relevant variables. Matching is an attempt to eliminate these variables as an explanation for the differences between the intervention and control/contrast groups. One must match on variables that are known to have an impact upon the outcome. For example, if the outcome variable to be measured is alcohol and other drug (AOD) use, one might match the experimental and comparison group subjects on age and gender since both impact upon substance use. It is important to recognize that one can only match on a limited number of variables since it is often hard to find a matching case for the contrast group. If one is matching for age and gender and one has a thirteen-year-old female in the experimental group, it is necessary to have a thirteen-year-old female in the control/contrast group. If a match is not found, the experimental subject must be dropped from the analysis. Every time one drops a subject, it distorts the findings to some extent.

Still another approach involves comparing post-test finding with data on the results for a similar group for whom data already is available. For example, one might compare your findings on school absenteeism with those of the district at large.

MEASURING CHANGE

Measuring change involves a delineation of what the program is meant to achieve and the selection, or development of, measures which tap that change. While in a laboratory experiment it is clear exactly what type of change one wishes to achieve, broad-ranging prevention programs may be designed to have a whole variety of impacts. For example, a program may be designed to increase parent-child communication, increase school bonding, impact self-esteem, change the behavior of teachers, etc. It is important that each impact be measured. If one can obtain measures that have been tested for reliability and validity and are known to tap the area the program is to impact, it is always preferable to use them since the development of reliable and valid measures is a time-consuming task. Adequate measures exist in many areas, including self-esteem and child behavior.

USE OF PRE-TEST DATA

There is a need for pre-intervention data to enable one to look at the degree of change in the subjects. Such data also enable one to statistically adjust scores in such a way as to eliminate the impact of certain extraneous variables. Sometimes the children can only be tested after the intervention. In such cases, unless the subjects have been randomly assigned to experimental and control groups, it is impossible to respond to the criticism that the two groups may have been different before the intervention.

There will also be times when one cannot develop either a control group or a contrast group. Pre-test data allow an analysis of whether the pre-test and post-scores reflect the expected changes and whether the degree of change is greater than chance.

IDENTIFICATION OF SERVICE PROVIDED

As noted above, in the laboratory experiment, it is possible to control the intervention with precision. This is hard to approximate in most prevention programs. It is therefore important that the evaluation includes a careful analysis of what services are provided, including by whom, to whom, with what frequency, and in what manner. The final aspect is most difficult since the services develop over time, so they often do not truly reflect the initial description of the program. The evaluator must begin by reviewing any materials that describe the services being provided, the purpose of each activity, what change in participants it is meant to achieve, and what techniques are being used to achieve the change. This information is important in the development of measures that reflect the desired change and enable the program to be replicated elsewhere. Knowing specifically what each service component is meant to achieve and exactly what is being done to create the desired change helps the program gain greater clarity about their approach. At a later stage it is important to knowledge building and the replication of the program in other settings. The evaluator will, on an ongoing basis, compare the actual delivery of service with the projected design. Ideally, this will involve the evaluator observing the program, but such an approach is time-consuming. He or she may instead review ongoing write-ups of the activities and/or meet with service staff to discuss what they do and why they are using particular approaches.

The evaluation process will be reviewed in greater detail below, beginning with means by which one gains a picture of what the program is meant to achieve. How and what should be measured will be discussed, followed by a review of how one determines whether the program achieves its objectives.

DEFINING THE OBJECTIVES OF THE PROGRAM

The first step in an evaluation is to define the goal of the program. In substance-abuse prevention, this involves deciding whether one focuses on preventing substance use or substance abuse. From a practical point of view, since use of all substances, including cigarettes, are illegal until age eighteen, most youth programs define any use as "abuse." Given that by eighteen a majority of youth have tried some form of drug, prevention programs must have the dual goals of not beginning to use as well as ceasing to use alcohol and other drugs. Different prevention programs target different populations and provide different services to achieve these goals. Among the possible targets of the intervention are individuals, families, schools, the legal system, and the community at large. For each target group, multiple activities may be undertaken. For example, one might provide parents with both a program designed to strengthen parent-child communication and a substance-abuse knowledge program on the assumption that parents who are knowledgeable about AOD use and are able to communicate with their children are more likely to have children who will not use drugs. Alternately a program may address increased police enforcement if its premise is that reduced drug availability will lead to reduced use.

The particular mix of targets of intervention and specific intervention approaches is connected by the overall theoretical framework within which the program operates. For each intervention there is, though usually it is not explicitly stated, a theory that links the program outcome to the activities being provided. Before outcome measures can be developed, the linkages must be made explicit. By now it should be clear that the first step is to define both what problem is being addressed and who has the problem. Those addressed may not actually be those with the problem but the two are linked on the basis of some theory.

Prevention programs may have three levels of outcome—immediate, intermediate, and ultimate. Thus far we have discussed the ultimate outcome of AOD use, usually referred to as program impact. Specific service interventions generally address more immediate outcomes. Thus work with parents may be designed to have an immediate outcome of more effective parent-child communication. The immediate outcome being sought is often referred to as "the result." The immediate and ultimate outcome may be linked by one or more intermediate outcomes, termed "the consequences." Again using the parent-child communication example, it is believed that the intermediate outcome of better communication between parents and children will be increased discussion of drug and alcohol issues and that parents will thus be able to help their children resist pressures to use drugs.

It is important to look at results and consequences because the ultimate goal of a prevention effort may only be measurable far in the future. For example, if a prevention program addresses children of alcoholics because of their higher risk of substance abuse in adulthood, the impact of the program will not be determined for years. One can however look at more immediate outcomes in terms of the degree to which certain protective factors, such as adaptive distancing, have been strengthened by the intervention. Because evidence shows that this factor differentiates between subsequent abusers and non-abusers, one may use this more immediate outcome as a way of judging the programs efficacy.

SERVICE OUTCOME LINKAGE

In the effort to specify the linkage between service components and outcome the reader will want to review each target of intervention and decide what specific conditions or behaviors they want to change or create. One will quickly become aware that some conditions cannot be changed by an intervention program. For example, a condition that places youngsters at risk of substance abuse is life in a poor urban community. This, unfortunately, is a situation that most prevention programs are not equipped to change. It is necessary, therefore, to explore what is different about those children in poor urban communities who do not become substance abusers. One such factor is the degree to which youth are bonded to the school. The intervention program may therefore target teachers with a program designed to help them be more available to the children in their classes. One would want to measure the immediate result of changes in the teachers' interactions with their students. One might also want at a subsequent time to measure the degree to which the students feel bonded to the school. At a later point one would want to look at whether these students are more or less prone to AOD use.

In developing an evaluation, it is helpful to complete a chart outlining the project. Chart 1 shows some (but not all) of the components of a substance-abuse prevention program. The ultimate outcome of all interventions is lower AOD use among the population to be addressed by the program.

Ideally, in defining how services are to be provided, the prevention program administrators and the evaluator would start by listing what the program is meant to accomplish and consider the range of ways the program can achieve those ends. From the range of options of targets and modes of intervention one would choose those best suited to the particular setting within which the program is imbedded. For example, a community center is likely to address a different population and develop different interventions than a school-based program. On the basis of such work the following chart can be completed.

In the case of an existing program, the process is somewhat reversed. One begins by listing what each program component is meant to achieve. One reviews the literature to see what evidence exists to support the linkages you have made between a given intervention and its presumed outcome(s). This is a difficult process because often programs are not thought of in specific terms. In an initial phase, the evaluator must analyze the specifics of what is being provided. On the basis of that work (which in the case of counselling would, at a minimum, explore the techniques used by the workers and the issues worked on in the counseling sessions), one would attempt to link specific aspects of the work to given outcomes.

In summary, the first phase of the evaluation process defines what the program is meant to achieve with each group with whom an intervention is planned and what specific activities are planned to achieve those outcomes. In developing a chart, one needs to remember that interventions have immediate, intermediate, and ultimate outcomes. The outcomes of each intervention should be listed in temporal sequence so as to be able to determine which outcomes can be examined over the life of the evaluation.

WHAT SHOULD BE MEASURED

Service Inputs

Often evaluations focus merely upon whether the projected change has been achieved. This is insufficient. One needs to define both the intervention (input) as well as the outcome. This involves detailing who is doing what, in what way, to whom, at what point in time. There are basically two aspects to programmatic inputs: The

Chart 1

Target of Intervention (who is addressed by service)
Specific Intervention (what is being done to cause change)
 Result (immediate outcome)
  Consequence (intermediate outcome)
   Impact (ultimate outcome)

A. Individual student
 1. Problem-solving training
  Ability to develop more alternative solutions
   Make more considered judgements about AOD use
    Lower levels of AOD use
 2. Informational sessions on alcohol and other drugs
  Increased knowledge
   Awareness of dangers of AOD use
    Lower level of AOD use
 3. Individual counseling of students using drugs
  Increased acknowledgment of AOD use problem
   Increase in percent of students receiving
   counseling for their AOD problem
    Reduced AOD usage

B. Parent
 1. Workshop on parent/child communication
  Increased ability to listen to and communicate with child
   Increase in number of talks with child
    Reduced AOD use by program youth

C. Teacher
 1. Workshop on identifying children with drug problems
  Increase in referrals of AOD using children
   Reduced AOD usage by program youth

first deals with the structure of the program, and the second the process by which the services are delivered.

The funding source often dictates whether more or less emphasis will be placed on structure, process and outcome. If the funding source is interested only in knowing whether its money has been spent as projected, evaluation might focus only on structural questions of staffing and resource allocation by reviewing the program design and what staff, equipment, space, etc., were proposed. On a chart like Chart 2, one would note the projected date of completion and actual date of completion of each component. Such a chart recognizes that during the start up phase different components would be in place at different points in time. One should also note whether the number of staff and their background and training are what were projected. Finally, note the projected number and type of treatment activities that have taken place.

Chart 2 does not deal with the issue of how the services are delivered, an issue that is impacted by the structures through which they are provided. For example, if an intervention was supposed to be provided by a social worker but it was actually provided by a teacher, the differences in role are likely to have created a difference in the services delivered.

Data on the process by which services are delivered are harder to obtain. What data will one collect and how will one collect it? One could include techniques used by the worker, topics covered, who raises what for discussion, or, on a broader level, the number of sessions, workshops, etc., conducted. In collecting only the later information, the evaluator assumes that the services were presented precisely as projected. A more micro-level analysis is usually preferable because very often services are not actually provided as projected, and different workers provide different services in very different ways. Micro-level analysis also provides an opportunity to gain considerable knowledge. For example, this writer was involved in an evaluation of mutual-aid groups conducted with children from families with a substance abusing member. In that study, the process evaluation established that the topics the children raised for discussion were related to the protective factors noted in resiliency research. Only by reviewing what went on in the group sessions was this unexpected finding identified. Micro-level analysis, however, is expensive and time consuming. One needs to be sure to cover the variety of workers and the variety of activities since both may affect outcome. In actually collecting the data, one will want to decide if observation, review of audio or video tapes, review of detailed script-like descriptions of what transpired, or meetings with staff is the appropriate way to collect process information in this setting. If one only needs to know that a given service was provided, a detailed process analysis is all that might be required. However, if one is concerned about the replication of the approach in other settings or with other populations, one does need a more detailed analysis.

Chart 2

COMPONENT			
Staffing	**Dates Hired**		
	Projected	Actual	Job responsibilities
Admin.			
Program			
Clerical			
O.T.P.S.	Date desired	Date obtained	
Equipment			
Space			
Intervention Program	Date(s) planned	Date(s) implemented	Attendance projected/ actual
Activity One			
Activity Two			

In summary, a good evaluation is concerned with the structure and process of the interventions as well as what those services achieve, thus, the need to collect data about frequency and nature of services provided, who provides the services, and how they are provided. Data about how a service was provided should be described in the context of the structures through which services were provided.

Service Outcomes

The measurement of service outcomes involves a series of activities. One must define the outcomes the program is designed to achieve so that variables to be measured can be determined. One must select reliable and valid measures of those outcome variables. One must decide when measurement should be taken, and finally one must decide from whom the data will be gathered. Each of these issues will be discussed in some detail below.

Defining the outcomes. As has been discussed earlier one begins by detailing exactly what outcomes each service is to achieve. The outcomes, as noted, can involve immediate outcomes, intermediate outcomes, and ultimate outcomes depending upon how long one anticipates being able to collect evaluation data and the questions that need answers. If one is not able to look at the ultimate outcome, one will need in the final report to be explicit about the linkage between the outcome measure(s) used and the ultimate outcome. This linkage must be supported by appropriate research findings. For example, if the ultimate outcome is AOD use, and school bonding the intermediate outcome, one will want to cite the literature that shows that children who are bonded to school have lower levels of AOD use.

Selection of measures. Having determined what outcomes to measure, one needs to decide what measure is suitable. While one can develop one's own measure, demonstrating that a new method is both consistent and valid is time consuming and difficult. It is usually easier to obtain copies of questionnaires used by other evaluators with information as to which questions worked well and which were problematic. One should also search the literature to identify scales that measure specific outcome variables. Many scales have already been tested for reliability and validity. A reliable measure provides consistent results when change has not occurred. Validity, on the other hand, deals with whether one is measuring what one intends to measure and only that. Below are detailed issues to consider in developing adequate measures.

Direct measures of behavior are usually more reliable and valid than indirect measures. However, while blood or urine testing is a more direct measure, there is considerable evidence for the validity of self-report of drug use. Further, an indirect method may be preferable because the measurement can be made immediately (as in measuring school bonding), while a direct measure may need to be tested at some point long after the end of the project. As a general principle in substance abuse prevention programs AOD use should be one measure of outcome if the youngsters are older than ten.

Usually the best measurement is empirically based. Measurement of behavior is always better than measurement of attitude. Attitudes provide a context for behavior but do not totally determine behavior. Thus many youngsters who will later use drugs will sincerely report they will never use drugs.

In selecting or developing one's own measurement tool, it is important to consider the age, developmental stage, reading and language ability of your data source. While persons rarely feel offended by simplicity, they are offended by measuring approaches that are too complex. Whenever possible, use a measurement tool that has been tested for reliability and validity with a similar population.

Scales have been developed by specialists to tap a wide range of knowledge, behaviors, and attitudes. Be aware that the meaning of words change over time, and words have different meanings to different subgroups. Even if modification is necessary, it will be better to start from an already existing scale then to originate one's own. In either case, examine that scale's reliability and validity. A number of techniques are available to explore reliability. They all look at the correlation between measures taken at the same point in time or at different points in time. The most commonly used reliability measure involves the calculation of the Cronbach Alpha. One desires a result larger then 0.60.

Validity can also be tested in a number of ways. Face validity, one method of exploring validity involves the determination of whether other experts believe the items used in one's scales clearly reflect the studied variable. Other validity measures involve looking at the congruence of the results of a given measure with associated measures. Thus one's self-esteem score should correlate with the degree to which one is able to assert one's views.

There are several ways to locate already-constructed measures. The first is to review the compendiums of scales such as Kumpfer et al. (1993), Robinson and Shaver (1973), Shaw and Wright (1967), or Corcoran and Fischer (1994). Another approach is to use electronic data bases to search the key variables such as the N.A.S.W. Social Work Abstracts data base, available at universities and libraries. In this manner one will often discover how others have measured the variable of interest. Remember, in reviewing scales used by others, one must see whether they have been used with a similar population and what reliability and validity tests have been done. It is also important to determine whether the measurement tool is culturally sensitive enough for the particular sample.

Timing of measures. Generally the timing of the pre-test is not a problem as long as it is completed before the intervention begins. The timing of the post-test, however, can significantly impact upon findings. For example, if one tests drug knowledge immediately after a drug information lecture, one may only be measuring what the participants remember rather than information they have integrated. Similarly, if the post-test of 30-day AOD usage took place two weeks after the intervention the test would include behaviors that took place during the intervention period. In contrast, measures taken long after the completion of the intervention may be impacted by other factors not controlled in the study. Of course, the longer the time between the pre-test and the program ending, the greater the chance that other uncontrolled factors can impact the subjects prior to the intervention.

If it was not possible to take pre-test measures, timing issues are even more significant. There is a chance of assessing the program before it is fully operational. A good process evaluation will alert one to this problem because it taps ongoing changes, allowing an assessment of the stability of the intervention. In post-test-only evaluations, one collects data at one point in time and has no way of knowing if the subjects look better or worse than prior to the intervention. One assumes that one's intervention caused any post-test outcome. As noted earlier, a comparison of the findings to existing data about a comparison group makes one more confident that the outcomes were due to the intervention. For example, one might gather data on school absentee rate from a non-intervention school that is similar in terms of the socio-economic status of the neighborhood and the race of students and compare the results with those of the intervention school. In a multi-year intervention focusing on one specific grade cohort, one might test a grade which will not receive the intervention with one that will. The issue for all comparisons, whether involving existing data or contrast group data, is whether the intervention and comparison groups are similar in all respects other than the intervention. To strengthen the conviction that the groups are the same, one may want to collect data not only on the specific outcome variables but also on other variables (e.g., age, income, test scores) to show that the two groups are similar on other variables that impact AOD use.

Use of pre- and post-test measures. Measuring the outcome variables before and after the intervention allows one to see whether, and how, the subjects changed. If the intervention is designed to improve self-esteem by comparing an individual's self-esteem score on the pre-test with his or her score on the post-test, one can look at change. However, even with pre- and post- measures, unless there is a control group one cannot determine the significance of the change. For example, suppose that AOD use remained the same despite the intervention. This does not mean that the intervention is a failure. A comparison of post test scores with a contrast school may show that the AOD use is higher in the contrast school though the difference may be due to initial differences between the two schools or an unexpected factor impacting the contrast school, such as the introduction of a state mandated drug prevention program at the contrast school. The problem of controlling external factors suggests the need to keep track of events happening in the school and in the community that might impact upon the intervention. For example, a mayoral decision to target a neighborhood for increased police presence may impact the findings. The only way of determining that the changes in the intervention group are not due to such uncontrolled factors is to randomly assign subjects from the same pool of cases to intervention and control groups. Both groups would then receive the pre- and post-tests. In such a situation one might be able to show that while there was an increased AOD use over a multiyear effort among intervention subjects, the increase was significantly lower than the increase among the control group, indicating that what appeared to be a failure was really a success.

From whom should outcome data be obtained. A final issue in the area of measurement is who should be measured. While youth are the ultimate target, multifaceted programs addressing a range of populations tend to be more successful. In general, all populations (youth, their families, the schools, the community) for whom an intervention is planned should be studied. Changes in the school setting are often very important to success in programs addressing youth who are already using drugs. One may need to know if one's intervention with teachers made them more receptive to reintegrating the troublesome youth into their classroom or whether they continue to see such children as too disruptive. In general, data should be gathered for every intervention with each target group. This does not always mean the subject of the intervention needs to be directly tested. For example, if counseling services are provided youth, data on their behavior may be collected from counselors.

Sample size effects. When considering whom to gather data from, it is also important to consider the effect of the size of the sample. In any research, ethical considerations forbid investigators to put anyone at risk. Some samples could be so small that it is possible to identify who said what. Thus one must consider the effect of breach of confidentiality when reporting findings. Another problem of small sample sizes is that it is difficult to find statistically significant differences. If one subjects data to statistical analysis, one will want to try to have samples in which the intervention group and the control/contrast group includes at least 30 cases. With samples below 30 one may wish to consider the use of qualitative research methods that are more akin to the approaches used in collecting process data. Qualitative techniques are generally seen as providing a less rigorous evaluation. Patton (1988) has an excellent overview of qualitative research methods.

If, on the other hand, one has a very large intervention group, one wants to consider selecting a random sample of those receiving the intervention and collecting more extensive data for that group than would be possible if data were collected on all intervention cases.

TESTING THE ACHIEVEMENT OF OUTCOMES

The testing of outcomes is what most people identify as evaluation. To prepare an analysis of outcomes, evaluators will want to extend Chart 1 to reflect the projected outcomes of each intervention, the way outcomes will be measured, the results obtained on pre- and post-tests, the comparisons made, and the statistical tests used.

Such a chart is often completed by an evaluator prior to the implementation of the project to provide a graphic picture of the evaluation plan. An example of a completed chart for the intervention "Informational Sessions on Alcohol and Other Drugs" is found below. Chart 3 assumes the existence of a contrast group. In reviewing this example, the reader should be aware that since one looks at different levels of outcomes (results, consequences, and impact) at different times the "after" measures may take place at different points in time though the "before" measure will reflect the same point in time. Often the timing of the tests is also recorded on the chart. In this chart, an "x" represents data being collected or an analysis being performed. For the intermediate outcome, only post-test data were collected. For all outcomes statistical tests are possible.

The questions found in Chart 3 will be detailed below. As the reader will note, data on AOD knowledge levels were completed only on a post-test basis with the contrast group, and on a pre- and post-test basis for the intervention group. The data make possible two different analyses: a comparison of pre- and post- test changes for the intervention group alone, and a comparison of the post-test scores of the intervention and contrast groups. The first analysis answers the question, "has the level of AOD knowledge increased significantly among the intervention group?" The second answers the question, "are the post-test differences between intervention and control cases in the expected direction and not due simply to chance?" For the intermediate outcome, awareness of the dangers of drug use, which is measured by the number of dangers they can cite, only post-intervention data are available. The question being answered is whether the number of specific dangers the intervention group cited is significantly higher than the number cited by the contrast group.

In terms of the ultimate outcome of level of AOD use, data are available from both pre- and post-tests. This makes it possible to calculate change scores for both groups. The question now being answered is whether the reduction in DOA use is higher (or degree of increase lower) among the intervention group than among the control group. When and what data are collected will determine what questions can be answered. For this reason, such a chart is often completed prior to the collection of any data.

WERE PROJECTED OUTCOMES ACHIEVED?

One decides whether the desired outcomes have been achieved depending upon pre- and post-test measures; level of measurement; and whether a comparison group exists.

If one has pre- and post-test measures for both the intervention and comparison groups, one can (with interval-level scale score data) subtract the post-test score from the pre-test score for each subject. Having thus created a change score for each person, one can then calculate and compare the average differences in results for the intervention group and the control/contrast group.

Percentage comparisons can be utilized when one is working with nominal data. If the data were nominal in nature, such as whether

Chart 3

Expected Outcome Problem	Measure-ment Device	Outcome Data[1] Intervention		Control/ Contrast		Change Score
		Before	After	Before	After	
Increased AOD Knowledge	AOD Knowledge Test	x	x		x	
Aware-ness of Dangers of AOD Use	Listing of Possible Dangers		x		x	
Lower AOD Use	AOD Self-report	x	x	x	x	x

[1] Statistical tests of significance should be calculated for all outcome data.

a given substance has been used in the last 30 days, one would report the percent who have "not used" among the intervention and comparison groups. With pre- and post-test scores but no control/comparison group, one would use statistical tests to determine whether pre- and post-test levels were significantly different. Without such tests, a more appropriate representation would be the percent of children who improved, who stayed the same, and who got worse. If there are very few cases, one should report the number of cases in each group rather than the percentage since with few cases, a one-person change can create a large percentage change.

With only post-test data and a comparison group, one would report the differences in status between the two groups. Depending on the data, one might compare percents (e.g., percent of AOD use) or the mean scale score (e.g., family solidarity score) for each group. Once again, statistical tests would be used to determine whether the differences were due to chance.

With only a post-test and no control/contrast group, one's options are quite limited. One would first attempt to find national or subgroup norms to compare findings to. Since often one's population was uniquely different from national norms before the intervention, it is quite difficult to evaluate what the meaning of the post-intervention score is. For example, the sample may look slightly worse than the general population, suggesting a negative outcome, when, in fact, prior to the intervention, the sample looked vastly worse than the general population prior to the intervention. Ultimately, with only post-test data, even if national norms are available, one can only assume the sample improved and indicate the current situation. This may not always be as troublesome as it seems. If the intervention group was selected on the basis of a known status for example, where students were identified by their teachers as probable academic failures, and after intervention the children did not fail, a stronger case can be made for the efficacy of the intervention.

Thus far we have considered situations where the comparison is between the results at different points in time or between two groups. Some evaluations pose other types of questions for which other forms of analysis are appropriate. For example, one may want to know whether an increased number of counseling sessions leads to a progressive decrease in substance use. In such an analysis, one would create a graph plotting the frequency of substance use with the number of sessions children attended. It is important that the number of sessions each child will receive be determined in advance, since otherwise the graph may merely reflect the decision that intervention is no longer necessary or the dropout rate at different points in time.

USE OF STATISTICAL TESTS

Whether one chooses to present the data as percents, as number of cases, as average scores or as degree of change between groups, or between pre- and post-test scores for a single group, the findings lack certainty unless one can demonstrate that the differences found are not due to random chance. Statistical tests provide the probability that the difference found is due to chance alone. By convention, if that probability is 5 percent or less, the intervention has made a difference. The statistical tests used are determined by the question one is trying to answer and the level of measurement. Since a discussion of statistics is beyond the scope of this chapter, if an outside evaluator is not available, one should consult a person knowledgeable about statistics to identify the appropriate statistical test. The calculation of statistical tests has become quite easy due to the many statistical programs available for the personal computer. Among the most commonly used statistical software packages are SAS and SPSS, both offer a wide range of statistical techniques. Windows-based statistical programs are particularly easy to use and let one both enter and analyze the data within the same program. A computer makes it easier to conduct more sophisticated analysis, such as an analysis where three groups or the effect of another variable, such as gender, are being compared. The availability of someone familiar with the particular statistical software one is using is most helpful in conducting a more sophisticated analysis. However, a more sophisticated analysis is not always required, since often a simple analysis of outcomes is sufficient.

WRITING THE FINAL REPORT

No evaluation, however well done, is helpful to the field at large unless its findings are widely shared. This has implications for how the final report is written. In writing the final report, it is important to consider the audience. Since often readers of evaluation documents are not technically sophisticated, one should keep the report simple with technical backup available to those who want it, either on request or in the appendix to the report. For lengthy reports, an executive summary reviewing the major findings is essential. An evaluation report should begin with a statement of the question to be answered by the study, followed by discussion of the program, including the resources needed to carry it out, and the theoretical basis for the interventions. A discussion of what activities were planned and what modifications were necessary to implement the program is most helpful in alerting others to possible replication problems. The report would then present the findings in some detail. A more general summary of the findings, with an interpretation of their meaning, their implications for substance abuse prevention programming, and recommendations which derive from the findings would conclude the report.

CONCLUSION

It is important to note that while simple evaluations can provide significant information, the field of evaluation research is quite complex, and a chapter such as this can only review some of the issues involved in planning an evaluation. The bibliography that follows lists a variety of more detailed treatments of evaluation methods as well as sources of measurement scales. While a person skilled in evaluation is an asset to the evaluation of a program, one should not hesitate to conduct an evaluation because evaluation expertise is not available. Knowledge in the prevention field, as in other fields, is cumulative, and so all studies add incrementally to the general knowledge about how effective substance abuse prevention programs should be designed. For this reason, evaluation studies are an important ongoing part of service programs.

REFERENCES

Campbell, D.T., and Stanley, J.C. (1966). *Experimental and Quasi-experimental Designs for Research*. Chicago: Rand McNally.

Corcoran, K., and Fischer, J. (1994). *Measures for Clinical Practice*. New York, Free Press.

Hawkins, J.D., and Nederhood, B. (1987). *Handbook for Evaluating Drug and Alcohol Prevention Programs*. Rockville, MD: Office of Substance Abuse Prevention.

IOX Associates (1988). *Program Evaluation Handbook: Drug Abuse Education*. Washington DC: Centers for Disease Control, U.S. Department of Health and Human Services.

Kumpfer, K.L., et al. (1993). *Measurements in Prevention: A Manual on Selecting and Using Instruments to Evaluate Prevention Programs*. Substance Abuse and Mental Health Service Administration, U.S. Department of Health and Human Services.

Linney, J.A., and Wandersman, A. (1991). *Prevention Plus III*. Rockville, MD: Office of Substance Abuse Prevention.

Norusis/SPSS. (1993). *SPSS for Windows: Base System Users Guide Release 6.* Chicago, IL: SPSS Inc.

Patton, M.Q. (1988). *Qualitative Evaluation Methods*. Beverly Hills, CA: Sage Publications.

Phillips, M.H. (1995). An evaluation of services provided by ADAPP to high risk youth. (Unpublished manuscript.)

Robinson, J.P., and Shaver, P.R. (1973). *Measures of Social Psychological Attitudes*. Ann Arbor, MI: University of Michigan.

Rossi, P.H., and Freeman, H.E. (1986). *Evaluation: A Systematic Approach*. Beverly Hills, CA: Sage Publications.

SAS (1992). *SAS User's Guide: Basics*, 6th edition. Cary, NC: SAS Institute Inc.

Shaw, M.E., and Wright, J.M. (1967). *Scales for the Measurement of Attitudes*. New York: McGraw-Hill.

Smith, M. J. (1990). *Program Evaluation in the Human Services*. New York: Springer Publishing.

Suchman, E.A. (1967). *Evaluative Research*. New York: Russell Sage Foundation.

Webb, E.J., et al. (1981). *Nonreactive Measures in the Social Sciences*, 2nd ed. Dallas: Houghton Mifflin.

Weiss, C.H. (1972). *Evaluation Research: Methods of Assessing Program Effectiveness*. Englewood Cliffs, NJ: Prentice-Hall.

Weiss, C.H. (1975). Evaluation research in the political context. In E.L. Struening, and M. Guttentag. *Handbook of Evaluation Research*. Beverly Hills, CA: Sage Publications.

CHAPTER 8

Funding Substance Abuse Prevention Programs for Youth

Roslyn H. Chernesky

As interest mounts in substance abuse prevention programs for youth and as the breadth and diversity of resiliency enhancement efforts in prevention programming emerge, schools and agencies are likely to seek support for such initiatives. This chapter examines both foundation and government support in the area of substance abuse.

We first look at foundation funding in the alcohol and drug abuse field, giving special attention to the 1980s when there was a surge in foundation support. This historical context is a valuable comparison to later funding in the field in general but particularly to more recent foundation interest in funding substance abuse prevention programs. Government support in this area is then reviewed. We focus on federal grants to see what government dollars have been made available. We look to see if President Clinton's promise of a substantial funding increase in education, prevention, and treatment is being carried out, especially with the recent shift in federal power and priorities. The chapter concludes with some information and ideas that schools and agencies may use in their efforts to seek dollars to establish or support prevention programming for youth. Since it will be necessary for schools and agencies to prepare written proposals in order to obtain grants, we focus on proposal writing and the grant-seeking process, and offer some tips for those writing proposals.

FOUNDATION FUNDING

The nation's 35,000 independent and community- and company-sponsored foundations have traditionally supported agencies establishing new programs and operating or expanding existing programs. In 1992 alone, $10.2 billion in grants were given. In real value, the growth was 7.5 percent, the largest gain since 1988 (The Foundation Center, 1994b). Although the amount of foundation dollars represents a very small percent of agency budgets (estimated at 7 percent), the significance of foundation support is greater than the actual dollars given. Grants make it possible to pilot new projects, demonstrate alternative intervention strategies, and augment programs to client populations or in communities with unmet needs. Demonstration and research initiatives often depend upon foundation dollars in their early stages of development. Foundation support has an indirect impact as well. It can also legitimize controversial programs, promote less traditional or alternative agencies, and focus national attention on emerging issues.

Foundations tend to favor program development, especially start-up of different and innovative programs. Support for special projects, 41 percent in 1992, is much greater than grants to continue ongoing programs, maintain agency operations, fund buildings, or purchase land or equipment. Although most agencies would like general support for their programs and unrestricted funding for their operations, grantmakers continue to be reluctant to allocate dollars in this way. Foundation priorities can influence agency programming. For example, grantmakers can serve as a catalyst, moving an agency from providing direct client services to providing technical assistance to other organizations (Chiti, 1990). Recent foundation interest in agency collaboration and networking in the delivery of services has stimulated organizations to submit proposals that demonstrate interagency provision of services.

Grantmakers continue to support health and human services today even though foundations are increasingly hard pressed to respond to society's growing needs and stepped-up requests for support. Funding for health, human services, and education far outpaces overall foundation funding and contrasts with foundation support given to other fields such as cultural activities, international affairs, science and technology, and social science. In 1992, human services accounted for 16 percent of grant dollars and one-fifth of the number of grants. Health ranked second by grant dollars, receiving 18 percent of foundation grants, the highest level of funding recorded since 1989. Support for education remained strong. Education ranked first in grant dollars, obtaining 25 percent. It also ranked first in number of grants, obtaining 23 percent (The Foundation Center, 1994b).

Alcohol and Drug Abuse Funding in the 1980s

A detailed picture of foundation support for the alcohol and drug abuse field during the 1983-1987 period is provided by the Foundation Center in its benchmark publication, *Alcohol and Drug Abuse Funding: An Analysis of Foundation Grants* (Renz, 1989). This study analyzes the allocation of foundation grants using the Foundation Center's grants database. The database includes about 40,000 grants of $5,000 or more made each year and is compiled from grant reporting forms that are voluntarily submitted by foundations. To assure that all of the 100 largest foundations are included, the Foundation Center collects additional information from annual reports and tax returns. Although the source of data has some limitations, for example, the information is heavily weighted towards large foundations, and small foundations or foundations that award large number of grants under $5,000 are underrepresented, it is the most complete source of data about foundation giving.

The Foundation Center's alcohol and drug abuse study, which this section of the chapter draws upon, is based on 1,814 grants totaling $87 million over a five-year period. At the start of the 1980s, alcohol and drug abuse was ignored by all but a few private foundations. During the period from 1980 to 1987, when all foundation giving rose by 61 percent, support for substance abuse programs increased fourfold. As a share of overall foundation giving, alcohol and drug abuse funding more than doubled during the period, rising from 0.4 percent in 1980 to 1 percent in 1987.

Not only did the total amount of grant dollars for substance abuse increase, but the number of foundations giving in this area rose dramatically by over 77 percent, from 107 foundations in 1980 to 190 in 1987. From 1983 to 1987, 337 different foundations made 1,814 substance abuse grants totaling $87 million. Most of the 1,814 grants were small (2/3 were less than $25,000) and benefited local treatment or public awareness programs. Many of the largest grants ($500,000 or more) supported capital projects of nationally recognized treatment recovery centers, whereas grants over $100,000 supported not only treatment programs but national media campaigns, as well as school-based and community-based prevention programs.

Prevention programs, defined as school-based, community-based, and public awareness programs aimed at populations not classified as abusers, received 36 percent of foundation funding during this period. In comparison, intervention programs, which include counseling, treatment, and referral services as well as residential programs, received 48 percent of foundation funding. Prevention was the fastest growing area of foundation support in the substance abuse field. By 1987, prevention outpaced intervention programs for the first time. It received $13.7 million, or 52 percent of the grant dollars for alcohol and drug abuse. Intervention programs received $9.9 million, or 37 percent of the grant dollars. However, the actual number of grants for intervention programs was double the number for prevention initiatives. The largest share of prevention funding, 25 percent, supported school-based programs. Since prevention grants were aimed primarily at young people, more than one-third of all foundation substance abuse dollars—nearly $30 million—supported programs designed to reach and help teens and children.

Thirty-five foundations allocated three quarters of all the foundation dollars given to substance abuse. Yet, they funded less than half the total number of projects supported during the 1983-1987 period. The entrance of the Joan B. Kroc Foundation was a key factor in the tripling of grant dollars to the field. It became the single largest grantmaker in substance abuse, awarding $16 million from 1984-1987. In 1987, the Kroc foundation ended its funding commitment to substance abuse programs. Only one of the thirty-five foundations, the Christopher D. Smithers Foundation, devotes its resources solely to alcoholism. It is also the only foundation that has been continuously active in this area as early as 1952. Among the alcohol and drug abuse programs supported by the major funders during the mid-1980s were the following:

* *Project ALERT*, a model school-based drug-abuse prevention program designed by the RAND Corporation (Conrad N. Hilton Foundation)

* *Grantmakers Concerned About Alcohol and Other Drug Abuse*, a funding network addressing substance abuse issues (The Pew Charitable Trusts and the J.M. Foundation)

* *The Chemical People*, a public television special to combat drug abuse (The Metropolitan Life Foundation)

* *Medical Student Program in Alcohol and Other Drug Dependencies*, a program to enable educational institutes and summer schools to offer intensive education and training courses in alcohol and drug abuse to medical students across the country (The J.M. Foundation and the Scaife Family Foundation)

* *Hazelden Foundation*, a foundation to build multiservice facilities and develop new training and prevention programs (The

Joan B. Kroc Foundation)

  * *Marion County Schools'* substance abuse prevention program (Lilly Endowment)

In February 1989, the Robert Wood Johnson Foundation, the nation's largest health care grantmaker, announced the single largest commitment of private funds ever designated for substance abuse programs—$26.4 million for its *Fighting Back* program. The program's grants supported initiatives of local communities to develop strategies using education, prevention, treatment, and aftercare to combat alcohol and drug abuse. Communities were expected to consolidate resources and mobilize a critical mass of local leadership in order to reduce the demand for illegal drugs and alcohol. Fifteen communities across the country were chosen. Programs included efforts to combat alcohol abuse among pregnant women; to help those at high risk, like school dropouts; to train residents to fight drug abuse; to mobilize groups to develop preschool prevention activities in public housing projects; to offer economic opportunities to reduce the allure of the drug trade; and, to test the benefits of offering incentives to keep youth in prevention follow-up programs. Funding for *Fighting Back* has ended. As of 1992, Robert Wood Johnson's substance abuse funding intended to target teenagers and children, particularly focusing on alcohol and tobacco.

By the close of the 1980s, community foundations were compelled to respond to urgent drug problems in the localities they serve and, therefore, increased their support for substance abuse prevention programs. For example, the New York Community Trust, one of the nation's largest community foundations, established a formal substance abuse program focusing on prevention and early intervention for children and youth that has a fund devoted solely to it. Other community foundations similarly responded, including the Community Foundation of Greater Washington, DC., the Winston-Salem Foundation, and the Community Foundation for Southeastern Michigan.

In summary, it can be said that the substance-abuse field prospered with the help of the nation's foundations during the 1980s. Foundation support for alcohol and drug abuse programs more than doubled. As a share of all foundation funding, alcohol and drug abuse giving doubled, and the number of grants awarded annually nearly doubled as well. Despite its large percent increase, however, the field never obtained more than 1 percent of total foundation giving.

Foundation Interest in Substance Abuse Prevention for Youth in the 1990s

By the 1990-1991 foundation reporting period, foundation funding for substance abuse continued to rise. The Foundation Center lists in its 1992 *Grants for Alcohol and Drug Abuse* 677 grants of $10,000 or more with a total value of $41 million made by 278 foundations (The Foundation Center, 1993b). Of the 1990-1991 total amount, $14 million was allocated for 226 grants for children and youth. The largest recipient of substance abuse grants was mental health agencies, who obtained 344 grants worth $19.6 million. Schools, on the other hand, received only 11 grants with a total value of $650, 856.

To determine which foundations are interested in funding substance abuse prevention programs for youth, the 1993 edition of the *Foundation Directory* was consulted (The Foundation Center, 1993a). The *Foundation Directory* is a major resource published by the Foundation Center that lists more than 6,000 of the nation's independent and community- and company-sponsored (corporate) foundations. It summarizes the grantmakers' purpose, fields of interests, activities, financial data, and limitations.

By using three descriptors—youth, prevention, and drug/alcohol abuse—it was possible to retrieve the names of all the foundations that would consider funding substance abuse prevention programs for youth. The retrieval resulted in a list of 32 foundations. Seven foundations were then eliminated because there was no indication of a giving interest in substance abuse prevention programming for youth in their description of purpose and activities or in the programs or projects they reported the foundation had previously supported. A list of the resulting 25 foundations appears in Table 1. The list is striking in several aspects. First, the list is remarkably short. Second, more than half the foundations listed limit their giving to local geographic areas, some to specific states and others to counties or regions within states. Considering that company-sponsored foundations primarily give grants to agencies located in areas of community operations, the four listed here as funding nationally may have skewed the geographic distribution of foundation funding for substance abuse prevention. Third, only five independent foundations that support programs nationwide appear on the list. Of those five, only three were major funders in alcohol and drug abuse in the 1980s, whereas two are newer to the substance abuse field

(M.E.G. Foundation and S.G. Foundation).

Only seven of the foundations listed indicated a *funding priority* to prevention programs targeted to youngsters or early intervention in alcohol and drug abuse: Bernard Osher Foundation; the J. M. Foundation; Lechmere Corporate Giving Program; International Charities; Plough Foundation; Ray Foundation; and S.H. Cowell. For example, Lechmere clearly stated that its social action budget concentrated on prevention and intervention programs that reach youngsters before they become substance abusers.

The grantmaking program in substance abuse prevention of the Conrad N. Hilton Foundation continued to be limited to its commitment to *Project ALERT*, a school-based substance abuse program. The Foundation created the *BEST Foundation for a Drug Free Tomorrow* of Los Angeles to disseminate *Project ALERT* to elementary and middle schools and to be a catalyst to bring community forces together to help curb the use of drugs, alcohol and tobacco among children and youth. *BEST* helps communities accomplish their own drug prevention goals by helping them to orchestrate anti-drug messages to children and to rally support for local drug prevention programs. Each community is provided with easy-access, low-cost, and high-quality promotional and educational materials. In April 1993, the Hilton Foundation announced that it would give *BEST* $5 million over two and a half years for general operation support for *BEST* to develop and implement school-based drug prevention curricula for grades 2 through 8. Over 25 percent of the Hilton Foundation grants went to *BEST* in keeping with its preference to reduce the number of grants awarded and increase the dollar amount in order to have a greater impact on a problem it has targeted.

In 1995, the Foundation Center published its *National Guide to Funding in Substance Abuse* which contains entries for 530 grantmaking foundations and 75 direct corporate giving programs that have shown an interest in substance abuse. They have either stated that substance abuse was a field of interest or have actually given grants of at least $10,000 to substance abuse which were reported to the Foundation Center in the latest year of record. The *Guide* lists 695 grants for a total of $91 million. Although a similar analysis has not been undertaken of these grants to determine how many have been given to substance abuse prevention for adolescents, there is no reason to expect a subtantially different allocation pattern from earlier years.

163

Table 1. Foundations Interested in Funding Substance Abuse
Prevention Programs for Youth, 1993

Foundation	Type*	Local (L) or National (N)
Beazley	IN	L - VA
Burlington Resources	CS	N
S.H. Cowell	IN	L - CA
GATX	CS	L- IL
Conrad N. Hilton	IN	N
Illinois Tool Works	CS	L- IL
International Charts	IN	L - CO
Irvine Health	IN	L -CA
J. M.	IN	N
Johnson & Johnson	CS	N
Robert Wood Johnson	IN	N
Samuel S. Johnson	IN	L - OR, CA, WA
E .B. Kelly & E. Kelly	IN	L- MA
Lechmere	CS	N
Lockheed	CS	L - CA
F. McBeath	IN	L- WI
M.E.G.	IN	N
Northern Trust	CS	L - IL
Ohio Bell	CS	L - OH
B. Osher	IN	L - CA
J. C. Penny	CS	N
Plough	IN	L - TN
Ray	IN	L - AZ, WA
S.G.	IN	N
US Bank	CS	L - WA

*Includes independent foundations (IN) also referred to as private
foundations, company-sponsored or corporate foundations (CS), and
community foundations (CF).

THE FOUNDATION PICTURE

The nation's grantmaking foundations—nearly 37,500—continue to
distribute billions of dollars in grants. In 1993, the latest year of

reported figures, the combined giving of foundations exceeded $9 billion, spread out among thousands of nonprofit groups in education, health and welfare services, the arts, environmental protection, and foreign assistance. Human services continue to benefit from their ongoing commitment. Foundations supported human services such as substance abuse, aging, and criminal justice even though they have been increasingly hard pressed to respond to society's growing needs during the 1980's (Chernesky and Gutheil, 1994).

Foundations as a group are financially healthy. A bullish stock market in 1993 raised their combined assets to an all-time high of $177 billion. Foundations are required by law to pay out the equivalent of at least 5 percent of their assets each year. But in other years, foundation assets dropped as market conditions changed, forcing many to dip into their assets to meet their funding commitments. For example, the Ford Foundation's assets of $3.7 billion dropped to $1.7 billion over a three-year period and then rebounded to $6.5 billion by 1992 (Teltsch, 1994).

The picture of foundation giving in the coming years is likely to be less optimistic. There are already signs that the nation's economic condition, with its unstable financial market and inflation, will reduce assets of private foundations just as they have begun to deplete assets of company-sponsored foundations. Company-sponsored foundations have already experienced depressed giving. Corporate donations dropped almost 14 percent from the mid-80's and are not expected to ever reach the old level again. As corporations tighten their giving, more of their contributions are tied to marketing. Instead of spreading out their resources, companies are strategically funding projects and causes that enhance their image and publicity (Sweeney, 1994). Many leading independent foundations, experiencing the impact of the economy, started to limit grant budgets in 1991, whereas community foundations appeared to be better able to weather the recession. Nevertheless, the Foundation Center (1994b) estimates that giving will continue to rise.

A reduction in the total amount of foundation giving will not be the only source of impact upon agencies and schools and their success in garnering foundation dollars for their substance abuse prevention programs. Shifts in how grantmakers are actually allocating their dollars will also affect opportunities to obtain foundation support. Three such shifts are already noticeable. Foundations are now collaborating—banding together—to tackle problems. In many instances, the combined monies establish a new funding pool in response to a specific crisis or need. But the foundations determine *how* the funds will be used. For example, one newly created, combined pool of 12 foundations is targeted to house New York City's homeless adults with special needs, particularly people with AIDS, mental illness, or a history of alcohol and drug abuse. The grants are available only to enable community organizations with relatively small sums of up-front money to secure loans for housing projects. Among the foundations providing the grants are the Conrad N. Hilton, Ford, Rockefeller, Altman and Ittelson foundations (Teltsch, 1992).

In an unusual collaboration in 1991, the Justice Department and two private foundations, the Ford Foundation and Pew Charitable Trusts, joined in an $8 million program to curb drug abuse among adolescents living in high-crime neighborhoods. Several cities where a large percent of young adolescents are vulnerable to drug addiction will be selected for experimental programs. The successful programs will then be replicated nationwide. The foundations will focus on drug prevention by providing youngsters eleven to thirteen years of age with recreation and tutoring and by encouraging local groups to help young adolescents deemed at risk of becoming involved in using or selling drugs. While the foundations will provide services that are viable alternatives to drug and crime, the government's role will be to first rid the neighborhoods of violent offenders and drug traffickers and then to move on to economic development efforts, including housing and education, to strengthen the communities (Teltsch, 1991).

Even when not collaborating, a second change can be seen in the more active role foundations are playing in designating where they want their dollars to go. As a result of more focused grantmaking, foundation giving which tended to be more flexible is now constrained by foundation priorities and targeted interests. In some instances, this role will make it easier to approach foundations when there is a match between agency interest and a designated foundation interest. But it also places grantmakers in key positions to determine which of society's needs and problems ought to be given priority and therefore deserve to be supported. This function is thus taken away from service providers, who are likely to be in a better position to know. A third trend is toward larger grants for two- or three-year projects. Although this approach will be advantageous to grant recipients, in the long run, it will mean fewer recipients.

The combined effect of these shifts is that foundations will have an even greater and more influential role in the delivery of human services than they have had. In effect, foundations will be deciding not only whether the substance abuse field should be supported but what kinds of programs and which populations within the field should be targeted. Grantmaking, heretofore driven by grantseeker interests and initiatives, is more likely to be driven by interests and strategies of foundations. Foundations clearly are moving away from being reactive and responding to submitted proposals to being proactive and seeking partners among agencies and organizations to establish projects that meet foundation goals.

FEDERAL FUNDING

By the 1980s, agencies had grown increasingly dependent upon tax revenue for the funding of programs, primarily through government grants and contracts. With the new federalism of the 1980s, federal funding began to drop, despite increased need. One of the service needs that clearly emerged during this time of reduced governmental financing was substance abuse. A commitment to substance abuse prevention and treatment that accompanied the Clinton administration was quickly eroded by a shift in power, a desire to reduce the budget deficit, and a very different view of the role and responsiblity of the federal government for the health and welfare of its citizens.

Government Support in the 1980s

The federal strategy for dealing with the problem during the 1980s had two goals (Renz, 1989). Priority was given to efforts designed to reduce the availability of illicit drugs. The second goal was to reduce the consumer market for those drugs. Responsibility for the first was lodged primarily with the Departments of Justice, Treasury and Transportation whereas programs to reduce demand were located primarily in the Departments of Health and Human Services (HHS) and Education (ED).

The major federal agencies responsible for substance abuse treatment and prevention research are the National Institute of Drug Abuse (NIDA) and the National Institute for Alcohol Abuse and Alcoholism (NIAAA), which are both part of the Alcohol, Drug Abuse, and Mental Health Administration (ADAMHA) within the

Department of Health and Human Services. In 1986 Congress created the Office of Substance Abuse Prevention (OSAP), now the Center for Substance Abuse Prevention (CSAP), within the ADAMHA where responsibility for both alcohol and drug abuse prevention research and demonstration programs were combined in one federal agency.

Federal spending by all government agencies for substance abuse more than tripled during the 1980s. Almost 90 percent of federal spending was allocated to supply reduction, especially on law enforcement, rather than on demand reduction efforts such as prevention and education programs. In fact, federal support for demand reduction programs actually declined by 40 percent from 1981 to 1986. With the passage of the Anti-Drug Abuse Act of 1986, total federal expenditures climbed to nearly $4 billion in 1987 from just over $1 billion in 1981. The Act provided for almost ten times as much funding for prevention and education activities. This funding was designated specifically for state educational agencies to make grants to local school districts and to state governors for community-based programs. Additional monies were later authorized but not appropriated as a result of budgetary constraints. Even with this increased support for demand reduction, supply reduction continued to receive more than three-quarters of the total allocated. The Anti-Drug Abuse Action remedied this imbalance by giving demand reduction almost as much emphasis as supply reduction for the first time.

Federal Assistance

Federal support for substance abuse prevention programs for youth comes from several governmental legislative sources and is administered by several different governmental agencies:

* Drug-Free Schools and Communities Emergency Grants (ED)
* Drug-Free Schools and Communities Counselor Training Grants (ED)
* Drug Alliance Grants (ACTION)
* Substance Abuse Prevention Conference Grants (HHS/SAMHSA)
* Anti-Drug Abuse Act (HHS/PHS)
* School-Based Drug Abuse Prevention Grants (NIDA)

The Drug-Free Schools and Communities Act provides federal financial assistance for establishing programs for drug abuse education and prevention. This assistance is the major, if not the primary, source of drug education and prevention funding in school districts across the country although districts depend upon funds from other sources as well to operate their drug education and prevention programs. Since 1986, the Department of Education has distributed $1.1 billion to states, about 80 percent of the total appropriated under the act. The remaining 20 percent was used for grants to the trust territories, grants for teacher training, and various national programs carried out by the Department. Each year, the amount of funds distributed to states has increased. In 1993, the Education Department awarded about $17 million in grants under the Drug-Free Schools and Communities Emergency initiative. For 1994, it was expected to make about 30 awards ranging from $100,000 to $1 million.

States receive funds under the Drug-Free Schools and Communities Emergency act according to their share of the nation's school-age children and the number of those living in poverty. Each state is required to allocate the funds among state and local programs and give 30 percent to the governor for discretionary grant programs and 70 percent to the state education agency. School districts apply to their state education agencies for these funds. Applicants must demonstrate significant need for additional assistance to combat students' drug and alcohol abuse.

These grants are targeted for the development and implementation of comprehensive community-wide drug and alcohol abuse education and prevention projects for students who reside in most troubled communities within local education districts. The act specifies that funds should be used to supplement on-going or state-required drug education and prevention activities. Funds can be used for such activities as: (1) developing, acquiring, and implementing school drug abuse curricula, textbooks, and materials; (2) school-based programs on drug abuse prevention and early intervention, such as individual counseling; (3) family drug abuse prevention programs, including education for parents; (4) drug abuse prevention counseling programs for students, parents, and immediate family; and (5) inservice and preservice programs for teachers, counselors, and others in the community.

The Education Department's Drug-Free Schools and Communities Counselor Training grants offer state and local education agencies as well as higher education institutions and consortia of those organizations and nonprofit agencies funds for training counselors, social workers, psychologists, and nurses who are providing or plan to provide drug abuse prevention counseling and referral services in elementary and secondary schools. Funds can be used to establish, expand, or enhance counselor training activities. Of special interest is reaching children from families that are dysfunctional due to substance abuse or children with social problems that stem from addiction. Under this initiative, approximately 35 grants ranging from $50,000 to $150,000 were to be awarded. These grants have been very competitive. In 1992, only 33 of 299 Emergency grants, or 11 percent were funded, and 51 of 227 or 22 percent counselor training applications were funded (Education Grants Alert, 1993).

Drug Alliance Grants come from the Anti-Drug Abuse Act of 1986. They are funded through ACTION, the federal domestic volunteer agency whose policy is to encourage prevention education in the fight against drug abuse by mobilizing America's volunteer resources. The grants are intended to create or expand community-based volunteer efforts to prevent drug abuse among youths living in low-income communities or public housing neighborhoods. They are open to nonprofit agencies as well as schools and school districts. Schools and school districts are expected to collaborate with community agencies and business in developing projects. Of special interest are efforts that involve parents and/or youth service agencies, linking youths and volunteers in an ongoing relationship. Competition is great for these grants with about one out of ten applications funded. For 1994, ACTION expected to make about 20 Drug Alliance grants of up to $25,000 each. Unlike previous years, ACTION was only able to fund one competitive round that year since it did not receive funding for two competitions (Education Grants Alert, 1992).

The Anti-Drug Abuse Act of 1986 and 1988 authorized the Office for Substance Abuse Prevention (now the Center for Substance Abuse Prevention) to make competitive grants to eligible states providing for the establishment of community activities targeted at alcohol and other drug abuse prevention through education, training and recreation projects aimed towards high-risk youth and their families. The mandate also provided for CAP to administer demonstration projects with a community prevention emphasis as a strategy for high-risk youth. The first grantee project was the

Community Youth Activity Program (CYAP). These demonstration programs eventually expanded to 31 state grantees during the 1989-1992 period.

The Health and Human Services Department initiative in this area focuses its funding projects on conducting meetings and national conferences to coordinate, exchange, and disseminate information on preventing alcohol, drug, and tobacco abuse under the Substance Abuse Prevention Conference grants. About $2 million were awarded to 40 grants in 1994. Each grant ranged up to $50,000. There were three competitive rounds, and ten to fifteen projects were awarded each round. All agencies—nonprofit, for profit, and public—are eligible along with local and state education agencies and higher education institutions. The grants fund conferences, workshops, or other formal meetings that target both the general public and health service community and focus on knowledge dissemination, problem-solving, network building, technology-sharing, health promotion concepts and practices in preventing substance abuse among high-risk youth.

Of least interest and value to agencies or schools planning substance abuse programs for youth are the School-Based Drug Abuse Prevention grants given by the National Institute on Drug Abuse (NIDA). Despite its name, these grants are limited to scientific studies and empirical research of school-based drug abuse prevention and intervention strategies. Proposals for funding are expected from higher education institutions and their faculty or staff researchers from fields such as statistics, psychology, or sociology. Schools that wish to design, implement or evaluate innovative interventions or demonstration programs would need to collaborate with higher education institutions.

In 1994, federal support for substance abuse prevention for youth included the funding of one major new initiative that had been authorized under the Anti-Drug Abuse Act, and a half dozen smaller grant programs under the Anti-Crime legislation which appropriated funds to both Health and Human Services and the Justice Departments.

* Substance Abuse Prevention Demonstration Grants for High Risk Youth Populations (HHS/OSAP/SAMBAS)
* Community Schools Youth Services and Supervision Program (HHS)
* Family and Community Endeavor School Program (HHS)
* Ounce of Prevention Program (HHS)

*   Urban Recreation and At-Risk Youths Project (HHS)
*   Juvenile Mentoring (OJJDP)
*   Youth Gang Drug Prevention Program (HHS/CYF)

Giving substance prevention among high-risk youth top priority, the then Office of Substance Abuse Prevention (OSAP) announced funding for programs that tested strategies directed solely at the prevention of and early intervention against alcohol and other drug use. Unlike previous OSAP funding, the emphasis under the Substance Abuse Prevention Demonstration Grants for High Risk Youth Populations initiative is placed on rigorous conceptualization and design of projects and the evaluation of them. Approximately $14 million was made available to fund an estimated fifty awards to public state, local, and federal organizations as well as private nonprofit organizations such as community-based organizations, universities, and hospitals.

Schools and school districts were expected to compete for grants in 1995 and also in 1996 to combat and prevent crime. Grants to support supervised school programs and after-school activities are available under the Department of Health and Human Services' Community Schools Youth Services and Supervision Program ($26 million in 1995, $73 million in 1996). HHS will offer another $11 million in 1995 and $31 million in 1996 to local educational agencies to develop or expand academic and social development programs as part of its Family and Community Endeavor School Program. These grants could also support after-school activities, mentoring programs, and even homework assistance. A somewhat different emphasis is found in the Ounce of Prevention Program, which was first funded in 1996. This grant program is targeted to areas with high rates of crime, juvenile delinquency, gang involvement, substance abuse, and teen pregnancy. While it, too, would support after-school and summer education and recreation programs, projects are expected to be collaborative among community-based and social-service organizations that have a coordinated team approach to reducing drug abuse or gang membership among at-risk youths. A similar thrust in funding comes under the Urban Recreation and At-Risk Youths Project, which was earmarked for $2.7 million for 1996 for HHS grants to local education agencies and local government agencies coordinating recreation programs with crime prevention efforts. Here, too, there are opportunities to relate programming to substance abuse prevention.

The Justice Department's Office of Juvenile Justice and Delinquency Prevention will fund one-to-one Juvenile Mentoring projects sponsored by local education agencies and public and private nonprofit organizations that are directed at youths who are at risk of educational failure, dropping out of school, or are involved in delinquent activities. Among the $4 million for up to 66 grants that will be awarded, projects that discourage use of drugs are possible.

HHS through its Administration on Children & Youth & Families will also be funding planning grants to help communities and neighborhood groups organize into formal coalitions to develop five year plans that concentrate prevention resources on a specific isolated target area. Under this Youth Gang Drug Prevention Program, plans should articulate a vision for youth and include community-wide strategies designed to change the environment or circumstances which put youth at risk of unhealthy and destructive behavior.

As can be seen, federal funding opportunities change almost annually and shift in response to different administrations and Congressional interests. Yet interest in substance abuse prevention as well as treatment had solid support within the federal government.

The Clinton Administration

Whereas the Bush administration devoted 35 percent of its anti-drug budget to prevention and treatment, the 1994 Clinton budget proposed a sharp increase in spending for drug treatment and programs to prevent substance abuse. It proposed spending 41 percent on prevention and treatment, up 20 percent from the $4.5 billion Congress had approved the previous year. Yet, most of the $13.2 billion for anti-drug programs was earmarked for law enforcement, 59 percent of the budget.

In contrast to earlier federal funding support, the Clinton Administration also asked for close to $1 billion for drug treatment and education programs as part of an anti-crime package over five years. This initiative was generally viewed as a significant change in the way the nation would respond to the drug problem and a recognition that prevention and treatment had been underfunded. Thus, although law enforcement would remain a major part of the country's drug strategy, there was greater emphasis on treatment and prevention within it (Treaster, 1994a).

Despite its support for more funding for prevention and treatment, the Clinton White House did not go along with the recommendations of a Rand study, which it had partly financed. The study quantified the relative merits of treatment versus enforcement and concluded that "a dollar's worth of drug treatment is worth seven dollars spent on the most successful law-enforcement efforts to curb the use of cocaine" (Treaster, 1994b, 19). Using a conservative estimate of a 13 percent treatment effectiveness rate, the researchers concluded that by shifting money to treatment, cocaine consumption, while addicts were in rehabilitation and afterward, would be reduced. Despite this dramatic finding, the White House did not want to divert money to treatment programs from international and domestic law-enforcement efforts (Treaster, 1994b).

By 1994, it became apparent that the good intentions of the Clinton Administration would not survive the budget and allocations decisions that reflected a shift in power in Congress, deep spending cuts required of all federal agencies, and plans to consolidate many heretofore competitive grant programs into block grants for states. It is not yet clear how these decisions will finally affect the substance abuse field and, especially, funding for preventing substance abuse among adolescents. The trends, however, are clear. Efforts are underway to virtually eliminate their funding and shift the burden of preventing and treating substance abuse to the states. For example, the House Appropriations Committee proposed to eliminate the Center for Substance Abuse Prevention altogether and reduce support for the Center for Substance Abuse Treatment by nearly 15 percent, eliminating all but the block grant program. Just at the time that 275 mayors across the country are crying out for more federal support to address drug abuse, cities will be getting substantially reduced federal funding and will see the elimination of critical programs such as youth gang substance abuse intervention (ADA, 1995).

The Education Department received only $25 million from Congress for competitive drug-free schools programs but costs for ongoing projects and other commitments totaled at least $40 million. Congress provided less than half of what the Clinton Administration had requested to meet program needs. The consequences of this deficit will mean no 1995 grant applications, sharp cuts in all continuing grants, and cancellation of emergency grants. Further information can be obtained from the Safe and Drug Free Schools and Communities Division, Office of Elementary and Secondary Education, the U.S. Education Department, (202)260-3954 (Education Grants Alert, 1994).

In July 1995, the Senate passed a bill to merge the Safe and Drug-Free Schools program with other youth programs. In the meantime, House appropriations asked that nearly $500 million be cut from it, claiming that the Health and Human Services Department could provide the services within its substance abuse and prevention block grants. The bill (PL. 104-19) signed by President Clinton on July 27, 1995 rescinded $16 million from Safe and Drug-Free Schools.

Accessing Substance Abuse Prevention Funding

The picture of both foundation and public funding for substance abuse prevention programs suggests that there are dollars available although they are neither abundant nor easy to obtain. We can anticipate that many schools and agencies will be competing for the same funds. But, all across the country, there are indeed recipients of grants, and there is no reason why *your* school or agency cannot be one of those recipients. A discussion of resources and techniques for increasing the chances of obtaining grants concludes this chapter.

PREPARING PROPOSALS

Accessing any available monies will require schools and agencies to prepare written proposals. It is therefore valuable to demystify the proposal writing and grant-seeking processes. There is already a rich library on proposal writing that is designed for that purpose. A number of key references are listed in Figure 1. Each book presents a step-by-step approach to preparing effective proposals. Each guides the reader through the stages of writing, locating funding sources, and presenting proposals. At least one book should be at the finger tips of anyone who is expected to prepare a proposal for program funding. In addition, the grant writing training programs conducted around the country by *The Grantsmanship Center* continue to be a valuable investment for a school or agency anticipating proposal writing as a key activity. For those organizations in which there is no staff to take on this activity or where staff is unable to assume this responsibility, use of a consultant might be advantageous. College and university faculty, especially from the schools of education, social work, and human services, frequently are available to help prepare proposals.

Getting Started

There are two avenues to getting started writing a proposal once the need or desire for a program is apparent. One route is to respond to information about available funding that seems to be targeted toward the kind of problem or need the organization was already addressing with no external funding or wanted to address,

---

FIGURE 1. Key Books and Articles on Proposal Writing

Coley, S. M., and Scheinberg, C. A. (1990). *Proposal Writing.* Newbury Park, CA.: Sage Publications.

Geever, J. C., and McNeill, P. (1993). *The Foundation Center's Guide to Proposal Writing.* New York: Foundation Center.

Grantsmanship Center Magazine

Hall, M. S. (1988). *Getting Funded: A Complete Guide to Proposal Writing.* Portland, OR: Portland State University.

Jacquette, L.F., and Jacquette, B.I. (1977). *What Makes a Good Proposal?* Washington, DC: Foundation Center.

Kauss, T. A., and Kauss, R. J. (1990). How to qualify for a foundation grant: a sophisticated primer. *New England Journal of Human Services, x(1)*, 15-21.

Kiritz, J. J. (1980). *Program Planning and Proposal Writing.* Grantsmanship Center News (reprint).

Lauffer, A. (1983). *Grantsmanship.* Newbury Park, CA: Sage Publications, Inc.

Lefferts, R. (1982). *Getting a Grant in the 1980s.* Englewood Cliffs, NJ: Prentice-Hall, Inc.

Locke, L. F., Spirduso, W. W., and Silverman, S. J. (1993). *Proposals That Work.* Newbury Park, CA: Sage Publications, Inc.

Mayer, R. A. (1972). *What Will a Foundation Look for When You Submit a Grant Proposal?* Foundation Center Information Quarterly (reprint).

---

but could not because of limited resources. At times, upon reading about a funders' request for proposals (RFP), it strikes an agency that if anyone were to be awarded a grant for such a program, it ought to be them since they have the experience, expertise, and the kind of problem that the funder has identified as priority. Keeping abreast of funding opportunities is critical. Often it is only upon learning that support for certain kinds of problems, needs, or programs will be available that schools and agencies begin the proposal writing process. This route leads the agency to the Request for Proposal (RFP) process which is the main route to obtain government funding. More recently, large foundations have also issued request for proposals for awarding their grants.

The second approach leads to the world of foundation giving and is driven primarily by the commitment and desire of a school or agency to get a program started even when funding is not obviously available or accessible. Once the proposal is written, funding sources need to be found and persuaded to support the program. The search for private dollars takes time and persistence to succeed. It is a step-by-step process that includes researching and identifying potential funders, contacting and cultivating them. With either approach, it will be necessary to prepare and submit a proposal to compete for the funds and to be awarded a grant.

Proposals for Government Funding

Grants from governmental sources are awarded after funding is authorized by the legislative body and actually has been appropriated to the governmental agencies for the coming fiscal year. The governmental agencies must issue a request for proposals (RFP), a request for concept paper (RCP), or a request for applications (RFA) which declares the parameters of the funding opportunity. Grants are awarded on a competitive basis and are considered for funding if proposals are:

* Submitted in response to the RFP
* Prepared exactly as requested on forms that have been devised solely for that purpose
* Meet the fairly straightforward set of criteria
* Correspond to the political needs, interests, and priorities of the government agency

There is no point in responding to an RFP if the organization or its intended program do not match what the government agency is seeking. For example, the organization would have to be sure it meets the eligibility requirements, which may limit recipients to certain kinds of organizations, auspices, and existing programs. The

RFP may require interorganizational collaboration, strong support and endorsements from relevant constituents in the community, or even involvement by community residents and intended program users in administering and carrying out the proposed program.

To best understand what the government agencies want, it is useful to be familiar with the legislative intent behind any governmental grant program. This information can be found in legislative committee reports, public hearings about the programs, public documents such as *The Federal Register,* and in the specific rules, regulations, and guidelines drawn up by governmental departments or agencies responsible for administering the program.

Learning about governmental RFPs is essential. It is, of course, best to learn about shifts in priorities, changes in funding interests, or legislation that will lead to new grant programs as early as possible. *The Federal Register* is the primary source of the news of new and continuing federal grant programs. Not all organizations have ready access to *the Register,* and relying on *the Register* frequently brings news too late for many schools and agencies who require more time to prepare these proposals than is ordinarily given (sometimes only four to eight weeks). Therefore, schools and agencies are encouraged to get on mailing lists of the government agencies and departments that are likely to fund in their fields and to arrange to regularly receive grant information newsletters from a number of sources such as state senators, professional associations, or private operations. A number of periodicals for nonprofit organizations have announcements about RFPs for new or continuing programs. These newsletters can be valuable in locating the most up-to-date funding information. A sample of such sources is listed in Figure 2.

An excellent newsletter source for schools and school districts is the *Education Grants Alert,* a weekly report on funding opportunities for K-12 programs, available by subscription. The Board of Education of the City of New York issues the *Funding Alert* informing educational institutions of available government funding and even some private funding initiatives. Schools were notified by the *Education Grants Alert,* published on April 28, 1994, that the expected, new federal anti-crime legislation would contain grant opportunities that could be used for substance abuse prevention. Funds would likely be authorized for 1995 for a number of different possible grant programs aimed at at-risk youth, including *Ounce of Prevention* for areas with high rates of crime, juvenile delinquency, gang invovement substance abuse, and teen pregnancy.

FIGURE 2. Key Sources of Funding Information

Alcoholism & Drug Abuse Weekly
>Manisses Communications Group, Inc.
>P.O. Box 3357 Providence, RI 02906
>Phone: 88/333-7771

Alcoholism and Drug Abuse Funding Service
>Program Information Associates
>P.O. Box 26300, Honolulu, HI 96825

Corporate Giving Watch and *Foundation Giving Watch*
>The Taft Group
>835 Penobscot Building, Detroit, MI 48226
>Phone: 800/877-TAFT

Education Grants Alert
>Capitol Publications, Inc.
>P.O. Box 1453, Alexandria, VA 22313
>Phone: 800/655-5579

ERC Newsbriefs
>Ecumenical Resource Consultants, Inc.
>1843 Kalorama Rd., N.W., P.O. Box 21385
>Washington, DC 20009
>Phone: 202/328-9517

Federal Register
>Superintendent of Documents
>U.S. Government Printing Office
>Washington, DC 20402

Foundation Center Grant Guides and *Foundation Directory*
and *Foundation Grants Index*
>The Foundation Center
>79 Fifth Avenue, N.Y., N.Y., 10003
>Phone: 800/424-9836

Funding Alert
>Board of Education of the City of New York
>Division of Funded and External Programs
>Phone: 718-935-3264

Grants Action Newsletter
>New York State Assembly
>Communication and Information Services
>One Commerce Plaza, Suite 1125, Albany, N.Y., 12260
>Phone: 800/356-8486

Grantmakers Concerned About Alcohol and Drug Abuse
        Marni Vliet, Vice President
        Wesley Foundation
        151 N. Main St. Wichita, KS 67202
        Phone: 316-262-7676
Local/State Funding Report
        Government Information Services
        4301 N. Fairfax Dr., Suite 875, Arlington VA 22203
        Phone: 703/528-1000
The Grant Advisor/Deadline Memo
        P.O. Box 520, Linden, VA 22642
        Phone: 703/636-1529

On August 4, 1994, their readers learned that the Justice Department would fund school projects to support one-to-one mentoring programs for youth to reduce juvenile delinquency and gang participation that could include discouraging use of illegal drugs (Juvenile Mentoring). The May 16, 1994 *Funding Alert* apprised its readers of the Youth Gang Drug Prevention Program in which the Department of Health and Human Services, Administration on Children and Youth and Families, was seeking planning grants to help communities and neighborhood groups organize into formal coalitions to develop five-year plans that would impact on the environment, circumstances, and attitudes that put youth at risk of unhealthy and destructive behavior.

Establishing a professional network of contacts to share information about upcoming funding opportunities represents an important role and function for administrators and directors who hope to compete for scarce resources. The U.S. Department of Education has helped to foster networks. Its Northeast regional center for drug-free schools and communities   [(516)589-7022] provides information on substance abuse prevention to schools, community teams, and the general public and offers training, seminars, and a quarterly newsletter. The Department's recently published booklet can help schools cope with school safety and drug abuse, giving examples of how 79 schools have successfully created and maintained safe and drug-free campuses. *Success Stories '94: A Guide to Safe, Disciplined and Drug-Free Schools* is available free, (800)624-0100.

People-to-people contact and word-of-mouth information usually precede formal announcements. Moreover, this kind of information can be especially useful although there can be distortion, inaccuracy, and misinterpretation. It is through these networks that schools and agencies can learn that recently authorized monies are not likely to be appropriated in the coming year or what sounds like a new funding opportunity is really a renewal that is likely to be awarded to the prior recipient. To appreciate the value of being part of a network that shares such information, it is important to also appreciate that much of this information could not be formally announced, and therefore it is deliberately leaked through personal contacts with the intention of notifying others about the actual state of affairs. Many agencies have learned not to bother writing a proposal when the funding opportunity was not real. On the other hand, others have learned that it is best to confirm rumors before taking something at face value.

Proposals for Foundation Funding

Unlike government agencies, foundations will accept unsolicited proposals. Only recently have some foundations issued RFPs. Grants from foundations are awarded to organizations whose proposals:

* Persuade grantmakers that a serious problem or need exists
* Convince grantmakers that they know how to solve the
    problem or intervene to reduce the need
* Demonstrate that the sponsoring organization has the
    capacity to provide the program as proposed
* Show the foundation why it is in their interest to fund the
    proposal

Foundations specify the purposes and policies that guide their giving. Some will designate very clear priorities and interests for a given year as well as limitations on giving such as geographical areas, types of organizational recipients, or types of activities that will be supported. Other foundations may be less specific as to their funding preferences but, by examining the foundations' recent history as to what kinds of grants they made and to whom, it is possible to get a fairly accurate reading to know whether your proposal stands a good chance of being funded. This vital information about foundations is available from the foundations themselves and by reviewing the publications of The Foundation Center such as the *Foundation Directory* and the *Foundation Grants Index*. Of particular value to schools and agencies seeking foundation support for substance abuse prevention programs is the Foundation Center's *Grant Guides*, a series of computer searches: *Grants for Alcohol and Drug Abuse; Grants for Health Programs for Children and Youth;* and, *Grants for Mental Health, Addictions and Crisis Services*. Each covers most of the 500 largest foundations and 450 other private and community foundations that awarded grants in that field. Listing grant information by recipient, location, and subject, the Guides make it possible to easily determine overall giving interests of particular foundations. These important sources are available for purchase from the Foundation Center. They often can be viewed in public or university libraries but are always available for free public use in the Foundation Center's nationwide Cooperating Library Collection in all fifty states. Agencies can locate the nearest collection by calling 1-800-424-9836.

There are also periodicals that specialize in providing nonprofit organizations with the latest information about foundation giving. These include *Foundation Giving Watch*, a monthly report, *Corporate Giving Watch*, also a monthly report that limits its news and ideas to corporate funding, the *Grant Advisor*, and the *Foundation & Corporate Grants Alert*. Even the *Education Grants Alert* identifies private funding opportunities. Periodicals such as the *Alcoholism and Drug Abuse Weekly*, an independent newsletter, provides reports on national trends and developments in funding, policy, prevention, treatment, and research.

Laying the Groundwork

The groundwork for preparing proposals should begin even before funding opportunities are announced or a specific proposal is written. Since all proposals, whether for foundation or government funding, require the same kinds of information, it behooves a school or agency to get started by collecting this information, keeping it updated, and making it easily available when needed. It is not unusual to find proposals that failed to be submitted in time because essential information was out of reach.

School or Agency Profile. Any funder will expect the organization seeking funding to demonstrate that it has the experience and capacity to carry out the program as promised. In the proposal, the

Figure 3.
Information About Agencies or Schools Needed for Proposals

* Brief history of the organization—why and how it was founded, sources of funding, significant programs

* Current activities—especially innovative programs and those in the field or with populations for which funds are now being requested

* Newspaper clippings that cite the organization and its programs

* Testimony from community members or constituents, thanking the organization or praising its work

* *Curriculum vitae* of key staff likely to be involved in the proposed program

* A list of members of Board of Directors (if not on letterhead), and/or Advisory Committee(s) members

* Documentation of all ongoing efforts to systematically collect and compile data on client satisfaction with existing agency programs

* Annual Report

* Agency newsletters

* Documentation of IRS tax-exempt nonprofit status

* Audit statement

* Copy of affirmative action policy

organization must be able to convince the funder that it is competent and credible. If one thinks about funding as an investment, then it is not surprising that funders want to be sure that their grants will be used to implement programs as promised and that the organizations they select are, in fact, capable of fulfilling their commitment. Organizations that have never received a grant will have to work harder to prove their capability. Organizations that are anticipating programming in areas or with populations that are new for them will have to work harder to show that their experience is relevant. Figure 3 lists the information that should be collected.

Although much of this information may be requested and placed in the proposal's appendix, a narrative section of the proposal will always require the organization that is submitting the grant request to makes its case regarding its capability. Therefore, this narrative can be prepared ahead of time, periodically checked and updated as needed. For each proposal submitted, this boilerplate would be revised to stress the information that is most pertinent to the specific proposal request.

Target and Community Profile. Since it is likely that proposed programs will be targeted to specific population cohorts and/or communities and neighborhoods, information and materials ought to be collected that document who the population is and can justify that their unmet needs, service gaps, or problems warrant new programs and funding. In other words, the existing condition of the potential clients and communities that the funded program would change needs to be made clear. Although specific proposals for different programs will require somewhat different information, in general, the information listed in Figure 4 should be readily available.

The Proposal

What do proposals look like?

No matter what the length, where the proposal is going, or the reason for the grant request, proposals look very similar. They all must include the same components, and they must be clear and convincing. It is not surprising to see that there is a consensus about the components of a proposal. Proposals must have a statement of need, the intended objectives or outcomes, a description of the proposed program or project, a budget, and information about the organization that is requesting the funding and will sponsor and

Figure 4.

**Information About Community and Target Population
Needed for Proposals**

* Current efforts by organization to serve the targeted
population and community—programs, numbers served

* Community data—statistics from secondary sources
indicating numbers at risk, trends, projections, and highlighting
areas of greatest need (usually available from school boards,
local human service or legislators' offices, local, state, or regional
government departments especially planning and community
development)

* Organization's relationship to the community (other
than providing services)—community leaders who contribute to
organizational decision making; staff who participate in
community-wide forums, task forces, or coalitions; collaborative
efforts such as the community using school space or agency
xeroxing

* Findings from any initiatives conducted to assess
unmet client and community needs or gaps in the existing
provision of services

implement the program. Proposals do not have to be long. A one-page abstract, or a four page concept paper would cover the same
components. The Foundation Center recommends eight pages
(Geever & McNeill, 1993). Governmental RFPs tend to require many
more pages, but they almost always specify the maximum length of
each proposal section.

Thinking of the proposal components as questions the funders
will expect you to address is a useful way to view a proposal and its
major sections:

* **Why** funding is being requested; the need, problem, or
condition the agency hopes to have an impact upon if the funder
would support the proposal; the anticipated consequences if such a
program were not offered; what evidence exists that the need really
exists and is not just in the minds of the proposers?

* **What** exactly will be accomplished or changed if the proposed program is implemented? The goals and objectives; the anticipated outcomes (measurable) in terms of how program users will be different (better) after participating in the program.

* **How** the program will achieve these goals; methods, activities, and tasks that will be undertaken; what is the program's intervention strategy(ies) and the rationale for it?

* **Who** are your intended program participants? What eligibility criteria will you use to assure that you will attract those who can benefit most from your program? What mechanisms will you use to reach potential participants and to keep them in your program? What evidence is there that they will want to participate?

* **Why** should you be funded to sponsor or implement the proposed program? What's your experience, your track record, your organization's qualifications and capabilities?

* **Who** will implement and manage the program if funded? Who will be the key management and program personnel?

* **Where** will the program be located? Physical site; community or neighborhood; organizational location. Where will it be lodged on the organizational chart? In what department or division?

* **How** will you know you are doing what you said you would do? What kinds of information will be collected and what kind of reporting will be done in order to demonstrate that the program was carried out as proposed and in compliance with the grant? What efforts will be made to systematically assess the program in order to get feedback that can be used to improve the program? What data will be collected through an evaluation design to be able to conclude at the very end that the program in fact made a difference and accomplished its goals and objectives?

* **How much** will this all cost? How much of the funds will be used for personnel vs. program vs. administration? Where else will financial support be coming from? Are the reasons for all costs explained and justified?

* **What** happens after funding? Will the organization continue the program using other sources of funding if it has proven effective? How will others learn about this program and be able to benefit from the organization's experience in setting it up or implementing the program? What kind of legacy will be left?

What Funders Want

Funders are like wary investors. They must be convinced that their grant is a worthy investment that will bring approval and praise to them because of their wisdom in making the grant. They want to believe they are a step ahead of other funders with a clearer vision of the nature of problems and how to address them. They like to see themselves in the vanguard in discovering problems and new solutions to ongoing problems, but they don't want to be too far ahead. They want to be recognized as leaders in problem solving but they want to be sure there will be followers. They don't want to be embarrassed by finding out that it was a mistake to support a program or fund a particular agency. They do not like uncertainty, ambiguity, or risk-taking. If they happen to be adventurous and venture from their more routine approach, it is unlikely they will take a chance on everything new —maybe on a new problem, a new program approach, a new idea, even a new agency— but rarely everything new at once. There needs to be some basis for confidence that the grant should be awarded.

It is up to the proposal and the way it is prepared to assure the funder that it is wise to award the grant. The organization must first convince the funder that a significant problem exists that urgently needs their support. Second, the proposal must convince the funder that the idea the organization is presenting as a way to address the problem is a good one—based on a real understanding of its "cause," building on experiences of similar endeavors, feasible, cost effective, and potential pitfalls carefully thought through. Third, the proposal must persuade the funder that the sponsoring organization, which will administer the grant and conduct the program, knows what it is doing, is capable of taking on this initiative, and can be trusted to carry out the program as planned.

Therefore, it will be useful to keep the following tips in mind when writing the proposal.

* Be sure the problem, need, or condition comes across as compelling.
* Make a strong case for the urgency of funding, and especially from this funder.
* Emphasize the organization's experience and track record.
* Demonstrate that the organization has a competent staff and administration, particularly as shown in the quality

and presentation of the proposal itself.
* Clearly narrow down the problem and/or target population in order to intervene in a meaningful way.
* Show your familiarity with the field.
* Demonstrate your familiarity with other programs in this field, especially if they are addressing the same problem, and make a good case for why another program (yours) is needed.
* Be sure the program is neither too grandiose nor too limited.
* Focus on what makes the proposed program unique, innovative, or clever.
* Check that there is an internal logic and consistency between what you state as the problem, what you want to accomplish, and your plan for addressing it.
* Help the funder believe it is making a wise investment.
* Show there is a match between the funder's interests and this proposal.
* Explain the potential for continuing or replicating this program.
* Make sure your budget is realistic; don't deliberately over or under budget.

Preparing a technically competent proposal to submit for funding from either government sources or foundations is necessary to assure consideration in the competitive awarding of grants. The quality of the proposal, however, may not be sufficient for assuring that you will be awarded a grant. Many factors influence the grantmaking process and the final decisions. Because these factors must also take into consideration the proposal itself, we have stressed that aspect of the grantmaking process here. It is a good place for agencies and schools to get started if they wish to obtain financial support for their substance abuse prevention programs for youth.

Commitment to prevention programming is likely to lead to schools and agencies seeking external financial support for their initiatives. Especially during times of drastic spending cuts, as all levels of government attempt to address growing deficits and balance their budgets, it is unlikely that new programs will be started unless special funding for them can be obtained. That is why it is necessary for administrators to know about funding patterns and trends and to learn how to access whatever funds that are available. This chapter provided a picture of both foundation and federal funding in the substance abuse field in general but specifically for substance abuse prevention programs for youth. How to get started writing proposals was reviewed along with some ideas on preparing successful proposals.

Both federal dollars and foundation grants are there to be tapped. Obtaining them, however, will require hard work on the part of schools and agencies. At a time when public funding appears to be at its lowest point, foundations will expect even more proposals seeking their grants. Proposal writing will be more important than ever.

REFERENCES

Americans for Democratic Action (August 1, 1995). *Proposed Reduction in Federal Support for Substance Abuse Prevention and Treatment and Related Programs.* Washington, DC.

Baumgartner, J. E. (1995). (Ed.) *National Guide to Funding in Substance Abuse.* New York: The Foundation Center.

Chernesky, R. H., and Gutheil, I. A. (1994). Foundation grantmaking in the 1980's: how three human service fields fared. *Journal of Sociology and Social Work, xxi(2)*, 153-60.

Chiti, J. (1990). The impact of funding priorities: nonprofits and funders have their say. *Nonprofit World, 8(1)*, 17-22.

Education Grants Alert (December 17, 1992). ED's 1992 grant programs show range of competition, 2, 6.

Education Grants Alert (March 4, 1993). ACTION funds volunteer anti-drug efforts. 3(9), 1.

Education Grants Alert (December 15, 1994). Money shortfall plagues drug-free school grants. 4(49), 1,6.

The Foundation Center (1993a). *The Foundation Directory* (15th ed.). New York: The Foundation Center.

The Foundation Center (1993b). *Grant Guides for Alcohol and Drug Abuse* (1993/1994 ed.). New York: The Foundation Center.

The Foundation Center (1994a). *The Foundation Directory* (16th ed.). New York: The Foundation Center.

The Foundation Center (1994b). *Foundation Giving: Yearbook of Facts and Figures on Private, Corporate, and Community Foundations.* New York: The Foundation Center.

Geever, J. C., and McNeill, P. (1993). *The Foundation Center's Guide to Proposal Writing.* New York: The Foundation Center.

Renz, L. (1989). *Alcohol and Drug Abuse Funding: An Analysis of Foundation Grants*. New York: The Foundation Center.

Sweeney, P. (May 15,1994). Corporate giving goes creative. *The New York Times*, 6F.

Teltsch, K. (December 17, 1992). Foundations give $8 million to house New York homeless. *The New York Times*.

Teltsch, K. (August 8, 1991). U. S. joins two foundations to fight drug abuse. *The New York Times*, A17.

Teltsch, K. (May 2, 1994). Foundations are finding some perils in prosperity. *The New York Times*, B1, B5.

Treaster, J. B. (February 8, 1994a). President plans to raise drug treatment budget. *The New York Times*, B9.

Treaster, J. B. (June 18, 1994b), Study says anti-drug dollars are best spent on treatment. *The New York Times*, 19.

INDEX